KEEP YOUR WALLET OPEN AND YOUR MOUTH SHUT

KEEP YOUR WALLET
OPEN AND
YOUR MOUTH SHUT

Charlie Farrell

FALCON
BOOKS

Printed in the United States of America
10 9 8 7 6 5 4 3 2 1

ISBN 0-9642047-4-6

Cataloging-in-Publication Data

Farrell, Charlie
Keep Your Wallet Open and Your Mouth Shut/Charlie Farrell
p.   cm.

ISBN 0-9642047-4-6
1. Weddings   I. Title

PS3556.A763K4   2003
392.5-dc21   2002095148

BOOKS

221 Lincreek Drive
Columbia, SC 29212
803-407-6619

To Java and Jackson, our two black Labs, who remained unconditional true friends throughout my ordeal, even when they too had to sacrifice. Except for one occasion (explained later), they never complained and always listened, even when my opposing side would not. I am forever grateful.

Acknowledgements

In my first book, *Courage To Lead*, the acknowledgment section was longer than the first chapter. I'm not sure anyone read it. As in that book, a host of people gave lots of help in this one—editing, grammar, punctuation, artwork, cover design, ideas via e-mails, faxes, and phone calls.

I know you can't wait to read the first chapter, so I will just list them and say thanks again to some very talented and sharing individuals. One of the few 100% positive things in life is writing a book and coming in contact with wonderful people: Judith Felix, John Harbin, Porter Kinard, Sandra and Bob Waldron, Chuck Sookikian, Connie Patterson, Wilson Farrell, Steve Garris, JoAnne and Butch Barrineau, John Wilson, Barbara Shealy, Andrea Andrews, Bland Quantz, Bill Estabrook, Jim and Sheri Jester, Roy Brown, and Janet Bainer.

Three people deserve special mention. Bill Holverstott, a Marine Corps flying buddy who, at one point in our friendship, I didn't know could read and write, has a special talent for literature and set me straight in many key areas.

Pat Coate, a brilliant copyeditor, went way above and beyond expectations with suggestions and attention to detail. It is nice to know that some of the smartest book people live in my hometown.

My wife, Susan, a "Cooperative Type" (explained later), did all the computer work. After some early, understandable "reservations" about this project, she enthusiastically jumped in with both veils (we had one *extra!*) and contributed immeasurably from the perspective of wife and mother of the bride.

I gave them an unlimited budget...

and they exceeded it!

Fathers of the brides,
everywhere...forever!

wed·ding (wed´iŋ) **n.** **1:** marriage ceremony with festivities **2:** nuptials **3:** joining together **4:** celebration **5:** financial disaster

Introduction

Aldous Huxley wrote a book entitled *Brave New World*. After the experience of being father of the bride you can author a *New York Times* best-seller called *Strange New World*. This role, truly a once (hopefully) in a lifetime adventure, forges an imponderable mixture of mystique, amazement, amusement, agony, and hopefully at the end, a good dose of exhilaration.

As you temporarily pass to the "other side" and become a fraternity brother of Bill Buckner, Dan Marino, Phil Mickelson, Jim Kelly, and Al Gore—that legion of men who snatched defeat from the jaws of victory—you vicariously experience their darkness, that lonely feeling of being shunned by family members, pitied by friends, and eyed warily by those, such as Ava the pastry chef, to whom you become financially indebted.

As the opposing side storms the wall of your financial fortress, words such as practical, reasonable, frugal, common sense, rational, and sensible may, from disuse, self-erase from your cranial hard drive. Although this fate is a temporary "condition," you *must* experience it as a rite of passage for all FOBs.

This book, along with the award-winning KWOMS Society (to be explained in the first chapter), assures your safe passage through the wilderness. Keep it near. In the darkest hours it remains your companion, friend, and confidant that guides you safely back to a normal life.

I love my daughter, Allison, more than a perfectly executed high-g barrel roll attack. She married Mark Stewart, as fine a person as I have ever met. My wife, Susan, is a thoughtful, level-headed wife and mom. *But.* . . .

I can proudly say that I have almost returned to normal. You can do it too; it only hurts for a while. Good luck!

ten'ta-tive *a.* provisionl, exper-
mental
teniu-ous *a.* sparse, slight, unsub-
stantial
ten'ure *n.* manner or right of holding
real estate, office, etc.
te'pee *n.* wigwam
top 'id *a.* lukewarm
**term *n.* limit; limited period (as a
session of a court); word, expression; name for an idea or thing;
terms *n. pl.* conditions, arrangements; *vt.* apply a term to, name**
ter'mi-nal *a.* pertaining to or growing at the end or extremity; ultimate, final
ter-mi-nate' *n.* & *vt.* set a limit to,

dly, secular; per-

a. for a time only;
ly adv.
vi. appear to yield to
unstances
a. capable of being re-
pt, of defended
us *a.* holding fast apt to
stubborn; retentive (as of
y)

one who holds land or
ender another occupant
cnant

vt. move, be di
crate:
tic

One

If you lose situational awareness while your life
gets completely overwhelmed by the wedding
process, or if you have forgotten the meaning of an
important word or phrase, this chapter serves as a
handy reference for the acronyms and terms in this
book.

Boat/Airplane: That old saying that a boat is a
hole in the water into which you keep pouring money
applies to airplanes and weddings. When you see
"Boat/Airplane," you know it refers to a portion of
never-ending expenses.

BOB: Brother of the Bride.

Budget: A meaningless number blown by at the spending rate of a jet fighter at mach two, flown by a young lieutenant with his hair on fire, heading toward downtown Baghdad to pay a little "social call" on Saddam Hussein. A first cousin of the "wedding balance sheet," a real oxymoron, nothing in this deal balances. Picture a beam with the wedding on one end and all of your money on the other end. The best you can hope for is that the wedding end won't bust a hole in your newly installed Mexican tile floor when it comes crashing down. The opposing side may develop such a distaste for being tied to a budget that they can't even say the word and may start referring to it as the "B word."

FOB: Father of the Bride.

FOG: Father of the Groom. The only one held in lower esteem and consulted with less often than the father of the bride; FOG is where he usually resides during most of the gestation period—a real noncombatant.

Gestation Period: The time between your daughter's engagement and her wedding day that starts the moment the young man asks "Will you?" and your daughter says "Yes."

Hassle Factor Index: Graph showing the relationship between spending money, decreasing fun, and increasing hassles during the gestation period. Explained in detail in chapter 4.

Hysteriamone 1: The wedding hormone released into the bloodstream of your daughter the moment she becomes engaged. One of the most powerful hormones on earth, it makes testosterone look anemic by comparison. The amazing thing about this hormone is its exponential increase in intensity during the gestation period, producing a feeling of euphoria with side effects of delusions of grandeur, loss of common sense, and an almost manic desire to spend money. A red flag indication of the presence of Hysteriamone: the bride refers to herself as "Princess" and, even worse, believes it.

Hysteriamone 2: The sister hormone of Hysteriamone 1, released into the bloodstream of the mother of the bride shortly after the engagement. Generally it comes on more slowly and with slightly less intensity than Hysteriamone 1 but has almost identical side effects—with one addition: a burning desire to shed a few pounds before the wedding.

KWOMS: Keep Wallet Open Mouth Shut

KWOMS SOCIETY: Brides' fathers who have banded together to do research and give moral support in this hour of need, the only outlet available for free frustration venting. Note: You could go to a shrink for $150 an hour, but guess what?—you can't afford it now, and besides, the shrink you go to probably doesn't have a daughter and has absolutely no practical advice to give you. Only fathers battle-tested on this "field of schemes" can understand and give you the empathy, comfort, and counsel you need. Joining the KWOMS Society delays onset of lines crossing in the Hassle Factor Index (fully explained in chapter 4). You may join the KWOMS Society by logging onto *www.charliefarrell.com* and then clicking on KWOMS. Please e-mail your ideas, funny stories, and unique toasts gathered during your darkest and most expensive hours since this type of communication has proven somewhat therapeutic in itself.

Line Accelerator: Increase in frustration or money spent, causing the lines in the Hassle Factor Index to lean toward a more vertical position of direct north or south, which shows lines closing at warp speed.

Line Decelerator: Decrease in frustration or money saved, causing the lines in the Hassle Factor Index to open. This may occur in some work situations such as a raise, promotion, or interesting assignment. No need to worry about this during the gestation period. Refer back to line accelerator and get comfortable with your new best friend.

MOB: Mother of the Bride. This acronym takes on a different meaning when more than two of the opposing side get involved in the planning of your daughter's wedding.

New York City Millisecond: Smallest amount of time known to man; the time in New York City between honking your horn and receiving the international sign of ill will.

Opposing Side: All individuals conspiring to bankrupt you; can include but not limited to your daughter and her sisters, mother of the bride and all her female friends, aunts, cousins, caterers, bakers, florists, musicians, ice carvers, limo drivers, dressmakers, photographers, and all other accomplices who have an out-of-wallet experience dreaming up ideas about how to spend *your* money.

Note: If you have a son, he most likely joins your side although not as a vocal supporter, having been forewarned by the opposing side that such services as good meals, clean clothes, transportation, and all other comforts of home may disappear if he gives any indication that he disapproves of a large percentage of his inheritance being blown on Sissy's wedding celebration.

SOB: Sister of the Bride. You may be mistakenly called this acronym along the way, likely a Freudian slip. They probably meant FOB and you can disregard—usually!

TRI: Temporary Romantical Insanity: Caused by a spike in intensity of Hysteriamones 1 and 2, this makes the person incapable of making rational decisions, especially about the expenditure of money.

Wedding Fever: Terminal case of spenditis.

Wedding Millisecond: Second smallest amount of time known to man; the time between when your daughter says "Yes" to the proposal and the release of Hysteriamone 1. This also signals the start of The Wedding Le Mans—"Ladies, start your spending!"

WPS (Wedding Probability Scale): Developed from extensive research by the KWOMS Society, this gives mathematical probabilities on certain events with a scale from 0 to 10. Here's how to decipher the 0, 5, and 10, all other numbers being gradients thereof.

0: Not a snowball's chance—for instance, the chance of having any money left after the wedding; otherwise known as zilch, scratch, nada, aught, nil, zip, zot, and naught.

5: 50/50—for example, the chance of declaring personal bankruptcy after the wedding.

10: Pretty much guaranteed to happen—for instance, the chance of the opposing side going over budget; otherwise known as sure-fire, lock, warranted, and incontrovertible.

$, $$, $$$: At the end of some chapters, one, two, or three dollar signs represent possible monetary risks. Whether or not you want to read this part depends a great deal on your tolerance for pain. The threat level description of each follows:

$: Low threat. You can read this without fear of raising blood pressure. The dollars associated here, although not totally insignificant, seem small—for example, the ring pillow.

$$: Medium threat. Distinct possibility significant dollars at risk. Reading this could put a real damper on your day, raise your blood pressure, and cause family and friends to steer clear—example, the wedding gown.

$$$: High threat. Net worth in imminent danger. Read this, which could inflict considerable physical pain associated with a foul mood, only if you are in great health; have an amiable, easy-come easy-go attitude; and have reconciled with the fact that this hairy behemoth (the wedding) has raced out of control—example, the cost of the reception.

Two

*I*f someone on the opposing side asks "Do you love me?" in a most sincere, genuine, and unpretentious manner, it may mean that the six-tier cake just smashed the budget to smithereens and she needs a financial bailout. Then again it may not.

Simple miscommunications cause a lot of misunderstandings and hard feelings during the gestation period. Consider the following sentence:

"I didn't say she lost the ring."

Pretty simple, and of course you understand what it means. However, look what happens to the meaning if you put the emphasis on different words:

I didn't say she lost the ring.
   (maybe someone else said it)
I didn't *say* she lost the ring.
   (maybe hinted it but didn't say it)
I didn't say *she* lost the ring.
   (somebody else lost it)
I didn't say she *lost* the ring.
   (misplaced it)
I didn't say she lost the *ring*.
   (lost something else)

The meanings of words, never in the words themselves, always come from our interpretation of inflection, tone of voice, facial expressions, and body language. Sometimes the opposing side takes our words and gives them erroneous meanings based on a fantasy that some distraught mother of the bride put out a long time ago that men can't communicate during the gestation period, or for that matter communicate in general. We world-class communicating men suffer from very bad press, especially on the listening side.

Most everyone has an internally wired communication filter located along the transmission line between brain and larynx. This filter traps errant, sarcastic, caustic, cynical, and highly charged emotional comments; it's an inborn relationship-saving mechanism that saves our bacon when we get really chapped. The problem in communicating with the opposing side during the gestation period occurs when Hysteriamone 1 or 2 temporarily clogs this filter. As fathers of brides we must recognize this, take the high road in communications, and accept the situation the way it unfolds, not as we want it.

Ninety-nine percent of the time communications about financial matters take place between you and the mother of the bride. You have a special relationship with your daughter that an unspoken rule compels the opposing side to do anything to preserve. Since negotiations over spending can cause volatile emotions and put strain on a relationship, the mother of the bride lets your daughter know that on money issues, "I will handle your father." Even though their tag-team spending would make the WWF proud, you may in fact go the entire gestation period and never speak with your daughter about money for the wedding. With the mother of the bride running interference, you at times feel like a Ping-Pong ball between mother of the bride and daughter as you endure long volleys, a few backhand shots with maximum english that go in unexpected directions, and then a smashing Wayne Gretzsky-type slap shot that ends the discussion. If you score three points out of twenty-one in this game, you rank above average, so this chapter primarily speaks to your communication with the mother of the bride.

Following are examples of comments you might make to the mother of the bride, her verbal and non-verbal responses, and an explanation on how to decipher what she really means. This information applies anytime in communication with women, not just during the gestation period; however, during the gestation period this "wedding-speak" is critical as you try to prevent the opposing side from nuking your net worth.

FOB: "Because of my golf game, I may show up about five minutes late to the party for Princess and 'what's his name'" (probably the fifth prewedding party so far for which you have sacrificed watching the Final Four, opening day of baseball season, or a complimentary Richard Petty Driving Experience at the Brickyard).
MOB: "OK."
TRANSLATION: If said quickly before moving on to another subject, it is *not* OK and therefore *not* acceptable for you to arrive late to anything that has to do with the wedding. The fact that *late* has replaced her maiden name because she made you late for the concert (Jimmy Buffett), movie (*Saving Private Ryan*), and dinner (with the governor) doesn't count.

FOB: "What's wrong?"
MOB: "Nothing!"
TRANSLATION: If said abruptly while turning and quickly walking away, big trouble brews (9.5 on the WPS). She will likely then wheel around in four steps, plus or minus one, quickly locomote straight back to you, grossly violate your personal space, point her finger between your eyes, and snap, "Since

you asked . . . !" (She probably overheard you tell a friend that because of this wedding your family needs to put the "fun" back in dysfunctional.)

FOB: "Anything wrong?"
MOB: "Oh, nothing."
TRANSLATION: If said in a normal voice, she, probably semi-mad, wants to tell you but wants you to dig for it. If you don't, she says you don't care.

FOB: "I don't think we need two limos. Why not let one make two trips? We ought to let the grooms-men walk the three blocks; some of them could use the exercise."
MOB: "Fine!"
TRANSLATION: If the word is spoken very sharply with tight jaws and teeth bared, it means, "This conversation just terminated, and if you say one more negative word about this wedding you just might wake up in the ER!" The best thing for you to do is vacate the subject and bring it up again later, when you just might get a "Well, O.K." with a small sigh (0.8 on the WPS).

FOB: "We need to call the hotel and cancel the valet parking. Let 'em park in the garage at their expense."
MOB: "Go ahead!"
TRANSLATION: If uttered with a hint of sarcasm and dare through thin, pressed lips, this means "go ahead" as in "GO AHEAD! MAKE MY DAY!" She

doesn't have the most powerful handgun in the world but wishes she did. Your best move: Extricate yourself as rapidly as possible from the Golden Retriever land mine you have stepped on.

If she says "Well, go ahead" in a hesitant but somewhat conciliatory tone, it means you have been granted permission to do what you want. She doesn't like it, but she offers you this one free pass. Just don't ask for something like this again. In exchange for this one free pass, payback follows, probably something like "Take me to the beach." (Refer to chapter 11.)

FOB: "Don't you think ice carving comes in a little pricey?"

MOB: "Give me a break!"

TRANSLATION: If said in a condescending and emphatic tone, it means she feels that you continue to attack her personally and criticize her spending judgment and good taste. However, she always follows up "Give me a break" with a full verbal counterattack and justification such as "This just shows your lack of sophistication. Anyone who can carve the Eiffel Tower with a Husqvarna 335 xpt 16 inch chain saw with decompression valve and inertia chain brake deserves appropriate compensation. Curb your chintziness . . . and keep idiotic thoughts like this to yourself! Besides, we don't want this incredible artist from South America going back home and destroying the Rain Forest, so as a bonus we help out with the ozone layer. I thought you believed in protecting the environment."

FOB: "Do you really need a new dress for the rehearsal party?"

MOB: Small sigh exhaled with pleasant face and calm demeanor.

TRANSLATION: Good sign. It could mean she has a handle on all the money being spent on the wedding and the new outfit she bought last month for girls' night out at the opera will suffice. Note this response (0.7 on the WPS) because you will see this very seldom during the gestation period.

However, it could also mean she's in a quandary deciding between the new dress and a carriage ride for the bride and groom. You have just made up her mind, and she's getting her Ph.D. in reverse psychology making you think you got your way.

If she gives a big inhale, big exhale, and big sigh with her head cocked to one side as she looks at you from the top of her eyes, it means, "You clothes-challenged idiot—of course I need a new outfit. This is *show time*! The two pounds I lost have rendered all my clothes useless!"

FOB: "Would you like me to call the baker and tell him to delete two layers from the cake and cancel the FedEx shipment of California strawberries?"

MOB: "Please."

TRANSLATION: When said in a normal voice, she offers a sincere thanks for your help or idea. Cherish this because, like the small exhaled sigh, you won't hear this very often.

If you get, "OH . . . PULEEEZE!" with the "eeeze" taking about three seconds, this translates as "You, the cheapest, most inconsiderate Dad since Archie Bunker, can forget that idea *right now*, like wedding millisecond *now*. We may have to pawn your autographed picture of Vince Lombardi hanging on the wall in your 'I Love Me Room,' but we ain't taking layers off the cake. Case closed!"

FOB: "Do we need a three-piece ensemble to play for the wedding? Wouldn't one violinist cover it?"

MOB: "Let me think about it."

TRANSLATION: This means no, but she doesn't want to say no because she hopes you forget about it. Or, in your nervousness walking down the aisle on the big day, she assumes (and you know what *assume* means!) you wouldn't notice the Boston Philharmonic playing "Stars and Stripes Forever."

Now that we have deciphered wedding-speak, it may help matters to pass along some communication tips to the mother of the bride so she can better understand you, the father of the bride. We can perhaps prevent miscommunications by being proactive in this area early in the gestation period.

Some of these suggestions came via e-mail from my e-Mafia, author unknown but probably some forlorn FOB on a mountaintop in Montana, banished there by the opposing side until summoned down on the wedding day to say the famous words, and *only* these words: "Her mother and I do." To think that only five words will be welcome from us during the entire gestation period, up to and including the wedding ceremony, is quite a humbling thought. Therefore, I present the following statements from FOBs to MOBs to open lines of communication.

- "All men see weddings in only a few colors. Stay with the basic rainbow and we can operate. Peach remains a fruit, not a color. Mostly we see green as in 'gone.'"
- "If you ask a question about the wedding you do not want an answer to, expect an answer you don't want to hear."
- "Sometimes, just occasionally, we don't think about the wedding. Ask us what we think about only if you want to discuss football, basketball, baseball, hockey, the stock market, or duck hunting."
- "Sunday means sports, *not* shopping."
- "Weddings will never make the Olympics; consequently, we have no passion for them."
- "*Whatever* you want to wear to the wedding I love, I promise."
- "We do not keep track of every special day. Please mark anniversaries on the calendar." (This gets heightened attention during the gestation period. Do *not* miss wedding anniversaries.)

- "Most fathers of the bride own three pairs of shoes. What makes you think we know enough to choose which pair out of thirty would look good with your dress for the rehearsal dinner?"
- "Come to us with a problem only if you want a solution. Please vent your frustrations about the wedding to your girlfriends."
- "Don't invite us to a 'chick flick' that depicts a young woman in love getting married. Except for films starring Clint (but scratch that one about a bridge), Arnold, or Bruce, we pass."
- "Anything we said two weeks ago about the wedding remains inadmissible in an argument. All comments become null and void after seven days."
- "If something we said about the wedding can be interpreted two ways and one of the ways gets you really upset, we meant the other one."
- "You can tell us to do something about the wedding or tell us how to do something about the wedding, but not both."
- "Please say whatever you have to say about the wedding during commercials, especially with the wedding six months away."
- "Beer excites *us* as veils do *you*."
- "Well, yes and no" remains a perfectly good answer to a question about the wedding.

I recommend when making these statements you use the word "we" or "us" instead of "I." The words portray all fathers sticking together. If one of the afore-mentioned statements strikes a particularly strong nerve with the opposing side (9.7 on the WPS), using "we" gives you an out by saying, "I didn't say *I* felt that way; I just read somewhere that most fathers feel that way."

And don't forget to insert their names into the message, as this tends to personalize and even soften the meaning. For example, when extending an invitation to a movie, rather than saying, "Would you like to . . .?" you should say, "Mary, would you like to . . .?"

Other great sources of information are telephone conversations you might overhear between the mother of the bride and your daughter. The problem is that you will only be hearing one side of the conversation, usually the mother of the bride's. Following is a one-sided conversation I tuned into about halfway through our gestation period.

> **Bride**: " . . . ? . . ."
> **MOB**: "Eight or nine."
> **Bride**: " . . . ? . . ."
> **MOB**: "That's correct."
> **Bride**: " . . . ? . . ."
> **MOB**: "Let's hope not."
> **Bride**: " . . . ? . . ."
> **MOB**: "Oh, I'm sure."
> **Bride**: " . . . ? . . ."
> **MOB**: "That would be great."

Bride: " . . . ? . . ."
MOB: "You bet."
FOB: "What was that all about?"
MOB: "Wrong number."

After a little "Sherlock Holmes-ing," here is my best guess of the real conversation.

Bride: "How much does the cake cost?"
MOB: "Eight or nine."
Bride: "Is that in hundreds?"
MOB: "That's correct."
Bride: "Does Dad know the cost?"
MOB: "Let's hope not."
Bride: "Do you think he'll be mad if he finds out?"
MOB: "Oh, I'm sure."
Bride: "Let's put it on my new VISA so he won't see it."
MOB: "That would be great."
Bride: "Does this put us over budget?"
MOB: "You bet."

To keep the information flowing you have to be careful when overhearing one-sided conversations that you don't give any indication that you are listening. Avoid eye contact, turn to the sports page or surf over to a ball game; the opposing side will assume, as usual, that you are not paying attention.

QUALMS VS. KWOMS

When I work with companies on creativity, one of the first concepts addresses how to respond to ideas. So often when managers get a suggestion, they fire back:

"You're nuts!"
"That costs too much."
"We've tried that before."
"That'll never work."
"You're not paid to think."
"Top management won't buy in."

Obviously, when managers respond this way the individual who gave the suggestion shuts down and becomes reticent about giving future suggestions, fearing embarrassment or being "put down" by a thoughtless manager. (Would you rather get 50% good ideas from someone who gives a hundred, or 100% good ideas from someone who gives only two?)

We always need to say, "That's a great idea!" This does not say we plan to follow through on the suggestion but in effect means, "Keep the ideas coming. Even though every idea might not fly, keep trying." Remember: Babe Ruth led the major leagues in home runs . . . and strikeouts!

Another statement you can make, "I have no qualms about that," assures you have no reservations about an idea which sounds reasonable. During the gestation period you hear lots of ideas which, let's face it, come up short. Others may be good, but their cost would cause a Three Mile Island-type financial meltdown. In a bind early in the gestation period, when checks are not yet being written, you don't want to squelch the enthusiasm. By the same token, you in good conscience cannot give your blessing to something that would cause your net worth to flame-out and dead-stick into a cornfield.

Let's suppose the opposing side invites someone to the wedding whom you don't think should be invited (9.6 on the WPS)—such as your daughter's Karate instructor, whom you haven't seen since your daughter finished runner-up to an Arnold Schwarzenegger look-alike in the under-sixty-pound class in the third grade. This one item won't send your net worth into a coma, but these things do add up (just wait till you read the chapter on "The List").

In this case you don't want to go to war and are keeping your powder dry for a more lucrative target, so you might consider saying:

"I have no *KWOMS* about that."

By this you mean, "I'm keeping my mouth shut, but I have never heard a more illogical, insane, and nonsensical idea. I can't believe you waste my hard-earned dollars on someone whose only positive attribute enables her to break two concrete blocks on her ex-boyfriend's head with her bare hands!" You, holding your ground and telling them what you really think, feel terrific, and the opposing side thinks you acquiesce. Try saying the following two statements quickly:

"I have no *qualms* about that."
"I have no *kwoms* about that."

I'll bet a bride's blue garter not one person on your opposing side hears the difference. Say, "I have no *kwoms* about that" with a smile and calm voice, and you know that your self-esteem remains intact. Your confidence puts you in charge and in control! You da man!

Sometimes living in denial is not a bad thing.

Remember, not only what you say but how you say it counts. Pick your spots carefully. Employ your best, most considerate low-key persona and watch the opposing side glow in the knowledge that they now truly understand the male psyche. They feel close to you, coming together in a spirit of teamwork, family, love, and understanding.

If you believe that last sentence, I have a business deal for you: some land along the Intracoastal Waterway near beautiful, scenic, historic, and Pat Conroy-written-about Beaufort, South Carolina, revealing itself, I promise, in two years max when global warming melts the polar ice cap and causes a

shift in the tides along . . . look, I need to be honest
here. We are doing all this great communication for
one reason—to survive almost certain fatal damage
to our net worth and Pickett's Charge on our sanity.
That women don't understand men (*Mars and Venus*)
and men don't understand women is exacerbated during the gestation period. Men look at this wedding
stuff by and large from a business perspective, while
women come at it from an emotional point of view,
so you might as well relax and enjoy another Moon
Pie and RC Cola.

* * * *WARNING* * * *

KWOMS Society research shows that the opposing side wants to eat out 314% more often toward
the end of the gestation period. Their reasoning, of
course, "I don't have time to cook because of all the
things I have to do for the wedding." This extra
expense "OF COURSE NOT!" comes from the wedding budget.

If the opposing side says, maybe after an exhaust-
ing afternoon of stuffing invitations, "Let's go eat
tonight at a place we haven't been to lately," you
must, no matter how difficult, overcome the powerful urge to say, "Let's try the kitchen." Saying this
gets you, guaranteed, a big inhale, big exhale sigh
with teeth bared, hands on hips, jaws tight, and head
down while cocked to one side looking at you with
wild eyes, "GIVE ME A BREAK!"

Three

*Y*ou ought to love this! The tradition in a lot of weddings has a precious kid all dressed up in his little ill-fitting suit or tuxedo walking down the aisle carrying a beautiful pillow with the rings on it.

When I first heard about this, I thought, "Well, even I know they're not talking about the pillow you sleep on, but surely they could use one of those nice little pillows off the sofa." You know the ones: small, of no practical use, and you have so many you can't sit down. We have a bunch of these really nice ones, darned expensive, made out of something exotic like velvet or silk that would do just fine.

But no! Wait a minute! Time out! Stop the presses! The ring pillow far exceeds your everyday run-of-

the-mill pillow. This special cushion, of utmost importance, must be created out of the finest materials,
handwoven by somebody with a name you can't pro-
nounce, and imported from some place you didn't
know existed, because it is the chariot for the symbols
of everlasting devotion!

Only one small catch here: The rings are not always
transported on this magnificent chariot the Queen herself would be proud to call her own, the focal point
upon which all eyes fix as it proceeds majestically
down the aisle. All your friends ooh and aah over
this angelic little crumb-snatcher, who is absolutely
terrified and probably thinking he would rather be
outside playing in the dirt, when the rings are not
even on the pillow! So why aren't the rings on the
pillow? They used to be, but after some exhaustive
research and battling with the Wedding Pillow Man-
ufacturers Association, who have tried desperately
to suppress this information for their own corporate
gain, here is the skinny.

It happened at the wedding of Miss Tiffany Nuss-
baum and Mr. Chris Madigan in Old Pond, Vermont.
The nephew of Tiffany, Jeremy Smackatella (later to
become Marine Corps PFC Smackatella), began cau-
tiously walking down the aisle of the beautiful little
Trinity Episcopal Church, with rings sparkling on
the pillow grasped firmly between his freshly wash-
ed hands—only the third time in history a ring pillow was used. It appears that Valerie Comstock, the
only bridal consultant in Old Pond and wife of the

owner of Velvet Pillows, Inc., came up with this idea to help sagging pillow sales. Anyway, little Jeremy, coming down the aisle, tripped slightly over one of the ribbons decorating a pew. One of the rings fell off the pillow and bounced under the dress of prim, proper, and slightly rotund Miss Eleanor Turnquist, sitting in the first seat of the third row behind the bride's family. Well, little Smackatella remembered strict orders from Dad, "No matter what, Son, get those rings to the preacher!" Being a great kid and demonstrating the gung ho, order-following discipline he would later show as a Marine, little Smack crawled immediately under her fluffy dress, so big it lowered the barometric pressure when she walked, and began rooting around for the ring.

This precipitated a most embarrassing turn of events, especially for Miss Turnquist, a spinster and retired third-grade schoolmarm who had taught three generations in this beautiful Vermont community. Not to mention that Miss Turnquist had not had anyone, shall we say, get in her knickers for over half a century. Quite a debate ensued for several weeks during the Monday Morning Men's Coffee Club at Mabel's Authentic New England Diner about whether she shrieked from terror or howled with delight!

Well, eventually little Jeremy found the ring in Miss Turnquist's shoe. He proudly brought the shoe out with the ring in it, providing further embarrassment because this proved that Miss Turnquist, who hammered her school children unmercifully on etiquette and manners, had failed to wear her shoes during the ceremony.

After the ring was found, the guests applauded modestly. Little Jeremy delivered the rings to the preacher, and the ceremony continued without a hitch. Since that time, as word spread in the wedding world, people have become really nervous about trusting their expensive rings to children. As a result, behind all the pomp and circumstance, the rings are usually in the pocket of the Best Man. Houdini would give an award!

The moral of the story: Be really careful about kids in the ceremony. They have the attention span of a Chihuahua and can direct attention away from the main attraction, which, let's be honest, features *your* daughter. This qualifies as one of those **kwoms** times.

$

If ever asked (0.8 on the WPS) which ring pillow you like best, you can bank some points that can be swapped in later. The question may concern your preference between an expensive beaded pillow and a less expensive pillow with ribbon. You should respond, "I think you should go with the beaded pillow because that is a really important item." If the difference, probably twenty bucks, constitutes a make-or-break deal with you, you need to find another game, my friend. Proceed directly to the chapter on the Hassle Factor Index while realizing that you, a minor leaguer in a major league sport, are about to be devoured like a snow cone on a hot Fourth of July. This is just the onramp of the expenditure super-highway.

You may be asked about things like this because, being small potatoes in the money department, the opposing side likes to be able to say among themselves that they have included Dad in some of the major decisions. Of course a 50/50 chance says your daughter ordered the pillow $400 ago. Other major decisions about which you may be consulted: colors of the candles in the men's room, whether or not the groomsmen should ride together from the church to the reception, and should the flower girls face right or left.

The reason you should pick the most expensive pillow is so that later you can say, "Well, since I gave in on the pillow, you can give in on the dress." Members of the opposing side in their morning war meeting have probably discussed the possibility of your pulling something like this, but it's worth a shot. You just never know in this gathering storm, but it might work and save you a few dollars on a $$ or $$$ item.

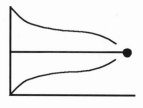

Four

When I left active duty with the Marine Corps I continued flying with the South Carolina Air National Guard. I noticed that for many of us the longer our careers lasted, the less fun we had and the more little things became annoying. I came to believe that joining the military just to fly airplanes equates to getting married just to have sex—you would have to put up with a whole lot of nonsense for a few moments of pleasure. This especially came true in the fourth quarter of our career.

Roaring down the runway on a crisp blue-sky fall morning with the afterburner belching 23,000 pounds of thrust remained just as big a thrill as way back when. But the other things—inspections, physicals, schools, formations, check rides, deployments, simulators, endless paperwork, briefs, and debriefs— caused the fun meter to dip. You kinda got that "been there, done that" feeling.

I had been cogitating about this premise for a long time but had not been able to get my brain around it and reduce it to a simple and concise blueprint that would show in graphic terms this conundrum of excitement vs. frustration, exhilaration vs. irritation, enthusiasm vs. disgruntlement.

One night after a six pack while watching Monday Night Football, I started to have a feeling I had never experienced—a bizarre blend of nervousness, expectation, and apprehension, as if I had just awakened in the middle of a wild dream. All of a sudden, as a blinding flash of light overcame me, my body went into contortions and propelled UFO-like off the couch into the middle of the room. My heart raced out of control, both arms involuntarily reached for the heavens, and I yelled at the top of my lungs, "Yes!! Yes!! Oh, my God, Yes!!" My wife happened to be walking through the room at the time. She didn't pay any attention and said later that I had acted like I always did when my favorite team scored in overtime.

Little did she appreciate the significance of that moment. At the juxtaposition of the hypothetical and true with karma at its zenith, the only colossal epiphany of my life occurred and I reduced this collection of fragmented thoughts to a coherent theory.

I can understand how Einstein felt that memorable night, sipping cognac and watching the stars with his lady friend from a balcony overlooking a charming snow-covered town square. Most cynics believe he had something else on his mind and that his most famous theory came to him much later that evening. Not true. It came to him much the same way it came to me, as $E=MC^2$. You just never know when flashes of brilliance might hit!

Unlike Einstein, my theory has not brought me fame and fortune in the real world. However, it did make me somewhat of a cult hero at our next Sunday morning drill when I presented my findings to twenty other slightly hungover fighter pilots, most of whom were starving for some insight into the meaning of life before they went out, strapped on the F-16, and cheated death trying to maintain the most important personal flying statistic of all—the same number of landings as takeoffs.

I have been awarded a Noble Piece Prize for this earth-shattering scientific concept, a little-known fact that my intellectual friends should appreciate. Dick Noble, one of our pilots and a real smart guy, along with two others and possibly a third who were mesmerized by my brilliant presentation jumped up and yelled, "Farrell, you piece of work. For this you get a prize!" Thus my distinct honor of being the first recipient of the Noble Piece Prize, a prestigious award that goes annually to the pilot who makes a major contribution to the local community, state, United States of America, Department of Defense, or the world at large. The latest recipient, a pilot who drank three beers in a row while standing on his head, disproved the primary theory of hydrodynamics, that liquid cannot flow uphill.

My theory, forever known as the **Charlie Farrell Hassle Factor Index**, being shared for the first time with the free world, convinces me that if you understand and internalize this concept, it will go a long way toward helping you through the financial apocalypse of a wedding.

The basic theory:

Over time, fun decreases at an increasing rate of decrease and hassles increase at an increasing rate of increase.

As I formulated this theory, it was meant to help my friends realize when they should retire from our reserve unit. Surprisingly, it has proven applicable in many different arenas. Look at the following graph. The line coming down represents fun, and the line going up represents hassles.

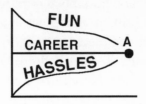

The key: Retire before the lines cross. Note that Point A represents the retirement date. If the lines cross after Point A, then no problem; you had lots of fun along the way and you exited at the right time with positive memories as you go forward remembering the "good old days" of flying with the eagles during the day and hooting with the owls at night. If, however, the lines cross *before* Point A, bad things could and usually did happen: restlessness, surliness, impatience, and short-term attitude.

As you run the final glorious laps of your gestation period you will see the same phenomena in action—fun starts decreasing at an increasing rate of decrease. More ominous is the stark realization of money being spent at an *increasing* rate of increase.

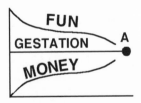

You *must* make it to the wedding, Point A, before the two lines cross, because if you don't, the graph proves that when the wedding happens you won't be having *any* fun and the opposing side has spent *all* your money.

It may be helpful to show KWOMS Society research into the movement of the lines and the possibility of the lines crossing prematurely.

Gestation Period	Chances of Lines Crossing
1 month	1%
3 months	8%
6 months	39%
9 months	78%
1 year	92%

With a gestation period that lasts over a year (known as an iwedarod) you would do just as well to pack it in. Get a good shrink, qualified banker, Dionne Warwick-approved psychic, and large supply of your favorite beverage (as Truman was advised) and hunker down.

$ $$ $$$

KWOMS Society research also shows possible cash outlay damage versus time of gestation period —sort of a financial Richter Scale.

1 month — insignificant
3 months — minor
6 months — significant
9 months — serious
1 year — catastrophic (as in a 9.5 on the Richter Earthquake Scale)

A wedding resembles bungee jumping from a 100-foot bridge over a river. You jump off the bridge with industrial-size rubber bands strapped to your ankles (the engagement). You free-fall headfirst toward the water (wedding), not knowing if this is a good idea after all, and about three-quarters of the way down the slack goes out of the rubber bands. You start to feel a tug on your ankles (wallet), your eyes pop wide open, and you cannot breathe as you reach terminal velocity (spending). A few feet above the water the bands go taut and your speed decreases rapidly like a jet fighter catching the wire on a carrier landing. Just inches from the water (bankruptcy) you come to an abrupt stop (the ceremony), and your body snaps upward, safe (solvent) when the bride and groom say "I do." You can breathe again, and you can now restart the life of normalcy you put on the shelf oh-so-many months ago.

The only remedy you have here as you say aloha to your moolah is to try and make the gestation period as short as possible. The obvious problem with a long gestation period is that it gives more time for the lines to cross and gives the opposing side excess time to figure out how and where to spend more money. If asked when the "big show" should be (1.2 on the WPS), to gain advantage say, "I can hardly wait. We just think the world of Jack, and I think you ought to have it as soon as possible, maybe in two or three months." (What you really mean is two or three weeks!)

Unless, of course, you don't like the guy your daughter intends to marry (don't let a fool kiss you or a kiss fool you!). In this case you want to length-en the gestation period, hoping the Princess comes to her senses and jettisons this ill-mannered, poorly dressed, unemployed, undereducated jerk-head who has greatly exceeded the low standards he set for him-self. Your fervent hope is that she reconnects with Tom, the bright, young, responsible orthodontist who probably remains madly in love with her. She canned him because he wears white socks, drinks Italian white wine, and listens to Pavarotti—in her mind all *very* good reasons to move on and hook up with Billy Bob, who hangs fishhooks on the "John Deere" hat he wears to the dinner table along with his imitation Oakleys. He thinks *Catcher in the Rye* plays baseball in Kansas. Ninety percent of his clothes come from the Bass Pro Shop in Springfield, Missouri, and his "nice stuff" from L. L. Bean. He doesn't know a car-buretor from a dangling participle, says "You know, man" at least once in every sentence and three times in a compound sentence, and ends sentences with the word "at" as in, "Where's the rehearsal party at? Where's the wedding at? Where are we gonna live at?" Answer: Behind the "at," you grammatically chal-lenged rhinoceros! Get a haircut and polish your shoes—they look as if you shined them with a Her-shey Bar and a rock! And, replacing the limo with a Hummer? NOT!

If you really like her young man and are 100% sure he deserves your daughter, and is the knight on a white horse whom you believe exceeds your extraordinarily high expectations, you want the trigger pulled as soon as possible. You might try these:

1. "I read somewhere that most successful weddings occur less than three months after the engagement. The extra time just confuses you, and someone as smart as you could probably beat that by a month."
2. "I read somewhere the economy may head south in a few months. Since the money for your wedding comes out of our mutual funds, you have more money to spend if you get married sooner."
3. "I always admired your ability to excel under time constraints. I read somewhere that brides like you plan a better wedding under pressure."
4. "Your goal in life has always been to have children. Every day you wait makes it a day longer until you experience the exhilaration of parenting."

Final shot: There may be 50 ways to leave your lover, but there's only one way to survive the gestation period: Make sure the big day arrives *before* the lines cross. Good luck.

My book printer said there are a couple of extra blank pages and asked if I wanted to add anything else. This gave me a great opportunity to pass along two other quality of life-enhancing theories, both first cousins of the Hassle Factor Index.

One is the brainchild of Bill Holverstott, a good friend and 767 Captain with American Airlines on the West Coast. This hypothesis came to him one afternoon between El Paso and Phoenix at 35,000 ft., exactly on centerline on a beautiful clear day. He had a full house, including Kobe Bryant of the Lakers, who had missed the team charter after a loss to the Mavericks and was licking his wounds in first class on the way back to LA to play the Bulls, 7:30 PST tip-off.

Bill had the airplane on autopilot and was preparing to update passengers on the flight progress when something in his left front pants pocket shifted upward, got caught between his lapbelt and leg, and started to pinch. He loosened his lapbelt momentarily after hearing a Pirep from another aircraft that they could expect a smooth ride for the next one hundred miles. He removed a key chain from his pants pocket to relieve the pinch. Bill looked at the myriad of keys, and just as he crossed Grand Junction with a Southwest 737 at his right two o'clock and two thousand feet below his altitude, in a moment of inspiration he formulated the **Bill Holverstott Key Theory**. So engrossed in this revelation, he never heard the flight attendant say, "Can you turn the heat up? Kobe is complaining about the fingers on his shooting hand getting cold."

His Key Theory postulates that your frustrations in life are directly related to the number of keys you possess. Look at your key chain right now, count the number of keys, and think about the purpose of each key and its associated frustration. Each key has taken on a life of its own, and like me, you probably have another bunch lying around somewhere and have forgotten where they all fit—your car, wife's car, kid's car, house (back, front and side doors), safe-deposit box, office (front and back), or the safe, gate, storage room, desk, locker at the gym, gun case, wine cooler, garage, lake house, "Uncle Jack's" temporary storage unit, lawn tractor, boat, neighbor's house—the list never ends.

You see men who have so many keys hanging on rings attached to their belts that they list to one side from the weight. Look into the face of any one of those men and see if you think he appears happy. Heck no! You never see a man like this with a smile on his face because he's got too many freakin' keys! He has hollow cheeks, sad eyes, a deeply furrowed brow, and an out-of-balance, key-induced limp. Those keys have sucked the spirit out of him like a prune on life support, and he wears a perpetual mask of frustration and hopelessness.

Bill's ultimate goal, after he's through flying, is to move to forty acres in central Oregon forty miles from nowhere and have only *one* key, the one to his green, camouflaged, extended cab, 4x4 pickup truck with gun rack, fog lamps, electric wench, Oregon

KWOMS

Ducks decal—and that key permanently welded in the ignition!

The other theory came from Bland Quantz, entrepreneur, inventor, classic car enthusiast, and raconteur—the **Theory of the Whomp Bird**. A little bird in Australia, the Whomp, at some point in his later years (note this happens to the male, never the female)—probably after the second flock of little Whompies—is overcome by the frustrations of life, probably bummed out at the unfairness in the competition for public recognition. Currently the Whomp Bird occupies third place for attention, behind the Koala Bear and the Kangaroo and only slightly ahead of the dreaded, overpopulating and royal-pain-in-the-derriere Jackrabbit (it appears, much to my surprise, that the Hassle Factor Index extends into the feathered world).

Once the lines cross, this beautiful little bird with gold wingbars and plaintiff song flies high into the sky and becomes impossible to see with the naked eye. It flies higher and higher until its perfectly configured, aerodynamically conformed wings stall in the thin air, at which time it tumbles beak-over-tail until the wings regain flying speed. It then goes into a sixty degree bank turn about thirty degrees beak low while accelerating faster and faster and at the same time increasing G forces in the turn as it nears max performance right on the edge of the envelope of controlled flight.

At approximately one hundred feet above the ground, as the bird's speed increases at an increasing rate of increase and the radius of turn decreases at an increasing rate of decrease, it reaches max performance. Much to the amazement of the Aussies on the ground, the bird flies up its own ass with a resounding WHOMP! . . . and disappears!

All your money meets the same fate, without the whomp!

SURE SIGNS THAT THE LINES ARE CROSSING

- The minister offers to take up a special collection for you.
- You stay at the Holiday Inn Express instead of the Holiday Inn.
- You bring home your half-used soap and shampoo from the Holiday Inn Express.
- When you read the *Wall Street Journal*, the word "insolvent" keeps jumping out at you.
- You start grilling out with Spam.
- You start making your own air conditioner filters out of towels from the ragbag.
- You put taps on the heels of your brand new Cole Haans.
- You can live with the knock of regular gas.
- You get two of the six handwritten thank-you notes the florist sends out per year.
- You look at the phone bill, $120 more than normal—all calls related to, but "OF COURSE NOT!" part of the wedding budget.

- You haven't talked to the opposing side about *anything* but the wedding for the past three months.

- You knocked your first hole in one and went home to tell your wife, "You can't believe..." but were cut off in midsentence by, *"You* can't believe what a great deal we got on a nine-tier cake." To this day she doesn't know you got a hole in one.

- Your wife's leased car, given to her last Christmas, went over twelve thousand miles in March with the wedding still eight months away.

- Your son comes home from college and shakes his head in amazement for hours on end without talking.

- Your banker asks for your home phone number for the first time.

- You request visitation rights on your bank account.

- Seeing cars decorated with "Just Married" makes you sweat profusely.

- The number of unsolicited credit cards starts increasing. One comes from Weddings-R-Us offering frequent flyer miles, a free simulated pearl and rhinestone tiara, and deferred interest until after the wedding.

- You have a recurring dream about standing in front of a bankruptcy judge in tattered jeans and T-shirt with a KWOMS logo.

- Seven bills come at once—three from Tiffany's, two from Neiman-Marcus, one each from Saks and Bergdorf Goodman. Afraid to open them, you have stopped going to the mailbox.
- You have heard the word "tonnage" several times in relation to the cake.
- That "previously loved" Yugo starts looking pretty good.
- VISA called twice to ask if the charge of $5,127.64 at the wine shop is legitimate. They have never seen one that big.
- You buy a lottery ticket for the first time in your life.
- You have started putting a "Do Not Disturb" sign on your wallet at night.
- You start rethinking "for richer or poorer."

As you look in the mirror each morning you see further evidence of the continuum of the **Hassle Factor Index**. A facial-pain scale developed through extensive research of the KWOMS Society follows:

Slight discomfort. Probably soon after the engagement when someone informs you the father of the bride pays for everything. Being a rookie and not knowing much about this sort of thing, you figure it can't be too bad. Lines in the Hassle Factor Index "get nervous."

Small Pain. While thumbing through *Reader's Digest* at the barber shop, you discover that the average cost of a wedding surpasses the price you paid for your first house. You are positive your opposing side is way below average in their thinking. Lines in the index begin to move.

Significant Pain. You realize your opposing side is way *above* average in their thinking. You pick up the phone at the same time your daughter does. The caller says, "I have some bad news on the cost of the dress you like." Your daughter, in a wedding millisecond, shoots back, "Sold!" Fun line turns slightly down and money line turns slightly up.

Extreme Pain. The opposing side talks in pig latin. You finally figure out what "Eway re-ay endingspay ayway ootay uchmay oneymay" means. You see the estimate on the cake. Fun line makes a sharp right turn, money line goes hard left.

Max Pain. An armored car comes to pick up the deposit for the reception. Your banker calls to inform you that your opposing side has placed a double order of checks and maxed out your overdraft protection. Lines almost vertical. Doubt creeps in that you can make it to the wedding before the lines cross. You have just entered wedding hell!

Don't get concerned when some of your close friends say you look tired, ask how you're feeling, or inquire about that new facial tic. You might return to normal a couple hundred paychecks after the wedding . . . have a great day!

Five

*Y*ou may remember that the theme song in the movie *Top Gun* was "Highway to the Danger Zone." Consider you are now entering the "Money Danger Zone." Wimps may want to skip this chapter; it takes a real man with nerves of steel to read this without knees buckling. Many a good hombre crumbles in a pathetic heap after learning what the opposing side has paid for approximately one hundred dollars worth of material, worn *once* in a lifetime. Magically converting one hundred dollars of material into thousands ranks as the number one smoke-and-mirror trick of all time—quintessential boat/airplane!

WE NEED TO TALK ABOUT THE DRESS!

First of all, this whole gown business is eerily reminiscent of women's fashion in general. A woman will stand before her filled closet and sigh, "Oh, woe is me I have nothing to wear," when almost all of its contents are new. She buys "new" when the skirt lengths go up and gives away the "old," donating it to Goodwill so she can help the less fortunate—sort of a Robin Hood complex. You plead, "Well, if trying to help the less fortunate, how about the father of the bride? I haven't seen you helping me lately!!" About the best you can hope for is a tax deduction of fifteen dollars for that two-hundred-dollar dress. She might even have a garage sale. (My advice: Do *not* go to your wife's garage sale; it makes you ill to see the markdowns on the original cost of goods.) Then the skirts go down, so she buys all new stuff, and we reenter the donation/garage sale phase. You can paint the same picture with blouses—this year ruffles in, next year out—and on and on it goes with slacks, shoes, belts, jewelry, hats, and handbags.

Now take a look at *your* side of the closet. What do you see? Unless you qualify as a real clothes-horse you see the same old suits, sport coats, white and blue shirts, slacks, and three pairs of shoes. Some of these have been hanging there for years—does regimental blue sport coat and gray slacks ring a longevity bell? I mean, what have designers done to men's fashion in forty years except come out with pleated pants? They try things like contrasting-color collars for shirts, double-breasted suits, and different-width ties, but men, way too savvy for this, keep these little fashion gimmicks from ever taking hold. Men know that even if they buy the new fad, they don't throw anything away because whatever style goes out will come back in soon enough and they will already have all the old "new" stuff. Besides, the three square feet of closet space allotted to the average man is plenty loose. Another one of the opposition's reasons for getting rid of clothes is "I have no more space. I told you four hundred square feet for a woman's closet doesn't get it!"

Here's one of those areas where the father of the groom comes out way ahead of the father of the bride. The best case scenario happens when the wedding is at three o'clock in the afternoon. The groom goes into his closet and grabs his one fraternity "uniform," a Sears off-the-rack Danny DeVito dark suit (he probably gets it cleaned for the first time since he had to go see the dean about academic probation his freshman year) and button-down 65/35 white 15 ½ x 33 shirt (he's grown three inches and gained thirty pounds since your daughter gave it to him three birthdays ago, but "it'll work"). Out-of-pocket expense: ten dollars for the cleaning and a dollar for the reattachment of the two buttons that he ripped off disrobing for the skinny dip at Lake Okatibbee at two o'clock in the morning while celebrating having passed Economics 301 and would therefore graduate in the fifth year of a four-year program, proving that it's possible to raise a 1.8 GPA to a 2.0 in one year of medium effort and minimum hours.

The worst case scenario occurs when the wedding kicks off at seven o'clock in the evening and the groom has to wear a tuxedo for the first time in his life. When your daughter mentioned "tux" to him he replied, "I promise to tuck in my shirt." If your future son-in-law is in this category, take heart; it only gets worse—probably when he walks down the aisle in his tux wearing white socks and Birkenstocks!

But in all likelihood, he goes down to the formal wear shop and stands there like a dummy while they measure him. He tries on the pants and coat, about a thirty-second operation, and pronounces, "Feels good to me." This is normal procedure when he buys clothes—never on looks, always on feel. On game day he returns to the shop and picks up his tux and accoutrements (he had never heard the word). Surely he has one friend, a father, or a brother who can show him how to dress, reassuring him all the way, "It only hurts for a little while, and you never have to wear one of these for the rest of your life." He hustles down to the nearest McDonald's for two double-cheeseburgers and large order of fries (he wolfs this down daily since one of his buddies convinced him it was full of Vitamin G!). He proceeds to the church, marries your lovely daughter, then heads to the reception where he spills *your* five-dollar-a-glass wine and *your* five-dollar-a-slice wedding cake on his tux (the latter happened when he and your daughter tried that "arm locking" contortionist maneuver and he got a white chocolate rosette smashed into his cummerbund).

He then leaves the reception and does a Superman-phone-booth quick change into his blue jeans and Dale Earnhardt T-shirt. He stuffs the tux, cummerbund, shirt, studs, cufflinks, tie, and shoes into a Days Inn plastic bag appropriated in Daytona during Spring Break. He leaves instructions for one of his buddies to return it to the tux shop the next day. He did pay an extra six dollars for loss and damage insurance, since his buddies, including the best man and three of the four groomsmen, are as responsible as a Cocker Spaniel on Prozac. Total cost with the insurance: ninety dollars. You can't touch that deal!

Let's compare that with the bride . . . "Rent a dress?! Heck no! The most important day of my life [stand by for a major hissy fit] and you ask me to wear a dress that has been worn before, probably by some hussy in a shotgun wedding, having the ceremony at ten thirty in the morning so if the marriage didn't work out it wouldn't ruin her evening. No self-respecting bride would *ever* wear a rented gown. I know you kid around a lot but please don't make jokes like that. I just finished my third panic attack worrying about the custom-made, diamond-studded, pearl-inlaid tiara from Paris getting here on time. The next thing I know, you'll want me to sell my dress after the wedding—NO WAY!"

$$ $$$

I hate to say it, but the die is cast. You *are* gonna get gowned. The opposing side absoweddinglutely wants a dress, an obscenely expensive one, even when they claim "inexpensive." After being worn once, the moths will say thank you for their fine dining in a Five Star restaurant for years to come. Or you can have it preserved and stored, which runs the cost out to about Pluto. If you overhear that the name on this crown jewel is Vera Wang, Christos, Versace, St. Pucci, Coutoure, or Pronovias, they have you wedged between a dress and a hard place. You might as well go ahead and sell your 1967 red Corvette convertible with big Stock 427 four speed, black custom leather interior, factory knock-off wheels, air conditioning, auxiliary hardtop, and side-mounted exhaust system. Your next door neighbor, eagerly waiting with cash in hand, has been coveting your prized possession ever since the engagement because he, a recovering father of the bride, knew you would cave in.

Women's clothes touch a very sensitive nerve, heightened during the gestation period as the visualization of floating down the aisle in a resplendent wedding gown makes Hysteriamones 1 and 2 pump with a little more enthusiasm. On the opposing side's scale of priorities the dress ranks number one, and they would eagerly sacrifice the Peking Duck and Three Kings Goat Cheese rather than give up the dress of choice. After having picked it out, spent hundreds of dollars in alterations, driven hundreds of miles for at least four fittings, had it boxed up, and headed out the door, their last words tell all: "Oh, how much do we owe?"

Just go ahead and submit to that gownectomy. It'll keep you from getting all hot and bothered when you hear 'em talking about the dress.

One more little tidbit to make your day—the new dress for the mother of the bride, which "OF COURSE NOT!" comes from the wedding budget. Her justification: "It can be worn elsewhere." Your reasonable response: "If that's the case, then something you already have can be worn to the wedding." You immediately get "GIVE ME A BREAK!" with head down cocked to one side, jaws tight, pursed lips, raised eyebrows, hands on hips, and breath of fire saying something about your socially deprived upbringing.

Six

*Please note that the pages in this chapter
do not have numbers.*

*A*lthough not an attorney, I attended a one-week
negotiation program at Harvard Law School
taught by Roger Fisher, author of *Getting To Yes*—a
terrific program, each day split between the theory of
negotiation and the practical application of the concepts through negotiating—one on one, two on two,
big groups vs. big groups. (By the way, if you think
this chapter recommends negotiating with the opposing side about critical expensive elements of the wedding, you can "fuhgiddabowdit." Negotiation does not
appear on their agenda as they spend all of your
money, and then some, without any input from you.
And no need to even mention other forms of dispute
resolution such as arbitration and mediation.)

One of the concepts we learned to use in negotiating is the power of legitimacy. For instance, let's say you want to build a house and the contractor gives you an estimate of $110 per sq. ft. You protest that this seems pretty high. The contractor produces a study researched by the local Chamber of Commerce (of which you are a member) that shows an average square foot construction cost for similar quality in your three-county area to be $112 per sq. ft. You think, "Well it's in line with the average cost so I guess we can proceed." In this case legitimacy convinced you.

Legitimacy can also protect you if, on the other hand, the estimated price from the contractor comes in at $124 per sq. ft. You have done your homework and produce the study showing average cost of $112 per sq. ft. Assuming similar construction, the contractor now has some explaining to do. You might also use this legitimacy technique when buying a new car. From the Internet you acquire the dealer's cost from an independent source and use this information in the negotiating process.

This powerful tool bombards us in commercials:

"As seen on TV"
"Over 1,000,000 people have tried . . ."
"Rated #1 by Consumer Magazine"
"Used by the U.S. military"
"As advertised in the *Wall Street Journal*"

These statements of legitimacy try to "prove" the value of the product or service.

Besides being in somewhat of a peculiar financial crisis with this wedding business, you have to deal with irrational people, so you have very few "normal" financial tactics available. Fortunately you still have the power of legitimacy as a weapon when you're reduced to the likes of a novice medieval pugilist tasked with defending the mother lode.

It's almost supernatural how three common words, in and of themselves so innocent, can, when strung together in the right sequence and delivered with passion, deliver such an emotional impact. No, these words are *not* "gimme a beer," "where's the remote?," or "what time's dinner?" The three most powerful words available to you during this financial crisis are:

"I read somewhere . . ."

You probably don't realize it, but think how often you have heard someone say, "I read somewhere. . ." or, just as convincing, "I saw on TV the other night. . ." or "I heard an expert say. . . " You and I have unconsciously used these phrases many times and never once thought about their implications. They provide instant credibility. Compare these statements:

1. "I predict below-freezing temperatures tomorrow."

2. "I saw on TV they're predicting below-freez-ing temperatures tomorrow."

Consider the first statement. What do you think would happen if you went home and said, "Honey, I predict below-freezing temperatures tomorrow so let's go out and bring all the plants in." You know what the response would be— "What do you know, the last time you forecast the weather we. . . ." See what I mean? However, if you went home and said, "Honey, I saw a prediction on TV for freezing tem-peratures tomorrow so let's go out . . .," your wife would zoom out the door at warp speed, wheelbar-row in hand, to collect the plants.

Powerful stuff this "I read somewhere," because you simply cannot say, "*I* think you ought to. . . ." Your opinion doesn't count! Accept that, but you can get your opinion across *and* accepted by the hypnotic power of legitimacy via, "I read somewhere that wed-ding consultants recommend artificial flowers." Take any cost-saving idea, attach "I read somewhere . . .," and you just sand-wedged to within two feet.

I have included some suggestions that you may be able to use. Remember, when you perceive anything disastrous to your financial well-being, just place these magic words in front:

"I read somewhere . . .
. . . that the groom should pick up half the cost of the reception."

. . . people notice when you use your grandmother's, mother's, sister's, aunt's, best friend's, or casual friend's cake knife."

. . . that because of the sugar content, brides substitute fresh fruit for large cakes."

. . . we should have just one flower arrangement at the church, preferably in a small vase."

. . . it's most fashionable to use the flowers from the church at the reception" (note the extremely persuasive word "fashionable").

. . . all fathers of the bride feel this way."

. . . that some misguided people don't like to go to weddings."

. . . our local super market was voted #1 in the state for wedding cakes."

. . . that we ought to consider a cash bar" (big possibilities here . . . BIG!).

. . . because of people driving afterwards, we should have the bar open for only one hour, or serve only beer and wine, or no bar at all. This protects our guests *and* what's left of your inheritance."

. . . that because of the high cost of gasoline, modern brides don't use limousines" (notice the word "modern").

. . . that the best time of day for a wedding is ____."
(Put in whatever time suits you, but weddings in the early afternoon can save you *lots* of money in *lots* of ways!)

Before the next "I read somewhere . . . .," picture this: A good friend of yours, a rabid football fan all his life, pays thousands of dollars each year for booster club dues and tickets and sits twenty rows up in Section G straddling the fifty-yard line. He tailgates every home game with ten of his closest friends, paints his face, wears school colors, and generally acts like an idiot for six home games a year. Do you think this man would *willingly* pass up Texas vs. Oklahoma, USC vs. UCLA, Ohio State vs. Michigan, Florida vs. Florida State, Auburn vs. Alabama, Nebraska vs. Colorado, or South Carolina vs. Clemson in favor of attending your daughter's wedding? I don't think so either, so for the preservation of your friendships you have *got* to encourage the opposing side to check the football schedule.

Suppose they don't check the schedule or, more likely, football games don't appear on their radar so they just don't count. As a result, your daughter's wedding falls on the day of a really important game. Your friend's wife applies the pressure and forces him to miss, in his mind, the most important game of the century. He lets you know it when you walk your daughter down the aisle: There he sits with an expression of disbelief on his beet-red sad face, portable radio earphone on, white knuckles squeezed as his jugular vein vibrates like a tuning fork. Cussing you unmercifully, even in church, he wants to know how you could be so stupid and inconsiderate to do the very thing he carefully chose *not* to do when *his* daughter got married. You have let the sacred brotherhood down, and he will *never* let you forget it! So, tactical nuke on the way to prevent this:

"I read somewhere about a big football game in town that weekend. Parking will be a hassle and hotel space impossible to come by."

This needs some amplification because of critical forces at play and precise navigation required. First of all you better catch this one early in the gestation period because it's one of the first decisions made, and once the date is picked, too late. There is no escape key on this deal, and it makes no difference if they find out a day later that the chosen date coincides with the start of Bike Week and 250,000 Harley drivers will blast by the church. Once they tell their first friend or relative a date, forget it.

Second, note that the emphasis is not so much on football, or any important sporting event that happens to coincide with your daughter's proposed wedding day. You must deflect the emphasis away from sports and onto the parking and hotel availability. If you paint a convincing picture that *one* person might not attend because of a problem with parking or hotel, you *will* get their attention, big time!

Critical point: Saying *you* think they ought to schedule around a football game, and you appear to be even a casual fan, you immediately get branded as a communist who has psychologically abandoned his family in the most important time of their lives. Remember, "I read somewhere. . . ."

I have to give credit to my opposing side on this one. Our two biggest football schools are the University of South Carolina and Clemson. They checked the schedules and picked a date when both teams had away games.

Some other days and events to steer the opposing side away from:

New Year's Bowl Games (December 31 — January 3)
Super Bowl Sunday (the whole weekend if you live where the team has championship possibilities; no sense taking a chance with 51 other weekends available)
Final Four (especially if your mascot is a Blue Devil)
Game Seven of the World Series
Masters Final Round
Kentucky Derby
Wimbledon Finals
Indy 500
America's Cup Finals
World Cup Finals
Daytona 500
NBA Finals
Shriners' Convention

Opening day of *any* season, as in duck, fish,
   deer, turkey, baseball, hockey

Valentine's Day (cost of flowers is out of sight);
   a wedding on Valentine's Day will give your
   net worth a dirt nap!

Here are a few more possibilities:

"I read somewhere . . .
. . . that meatballs are people's favorite."
. . . that for sentimental reasons you should wear
   the wedding dress of your mother, sister, aunt,
   great aunt, best friend, or casual friend."
. . . bad luck happens to the father of the bride who
   attends a bridal showcase."
. . . we should share the floral expense with the wedding that takes place before and after yours."
. . . really smart, cost-conscious brides are renting
   their dresses." (As a businessman you know
   that if it depreciates in value it's usually better
   to rent than own, especially for a onetime-use
   item like 99% of all wedding things; plug in
   any item here).

At the start of this chapter there was a note saying that the pages in this chapter do not have numbers; here's why: When you make the statement "I
read somewhere . . .," I guarantee you the first question from the opposing side, delivered in an immediate and rather sarcastic tone, possibly with hands

on hips and eyes narrowed, will be, "Where did you read that?" Since the pages do not have numbers you can truthfully say, "I don't know *exactly* where I read it, but it came from a book on weddings." And it's the truth! You don't know *exactly* where you read it, and it did come from a book on weddings.

In college I officiated high school sports—football, basketball, and baseball. Especially in baseball we learned to make calls instantly with 100% confidence and conviction. Can you imagine what would ensue if, on a close play at home plate between the Yankees and Mets the umpire said, "Hmm, I don't know, let me think about this for a minute." Oh man! Watch when major league umpires yell, "You're out!" No hesitation; they pump their arms and get their whole bodies into it. Even when wrong they act as if they're right. Also notice that as soon as they make a call they turn and walk away as if to say, "I've made the call. No questions. Let's get on with it."

Practice in advance for the time (8.7 on the WPS) when asked, "Where did you read that?" Look 'em straight in the eye and with sure voice and zero hesitation say, with confidence and conviction, "I don't know exactly, but it came from a book on weddings." Nod your head, turn around, and walk away with a million-dollar-saved smile on your face!

$$ $$$

Careful use of the concept of legitimacy can help release that chokehold on your net worth. However, like everything else, don't go to the well too often, and I would definitely not waste any of these on a $ item like the veil. A few more:

"I read somewhere . . .

. . . you should not bring shrimp in from out of state." (You can, of course, plug in any food or combination of food here.)

. . . you should have only one seafood and one beef."

. . . you shouldn't have seafood and beef together." (If you are questioned about "surf and turf," say, "That's a gimmick for the chain restaurants," emphasis on *chain*!)

. . . that flowers from a foreign country sometimes get held up in customs."

. . . that the practical, wise bride has the wedding in her home town."

. . . that artificial flowers help the environment."

. . . if you have more than three tiers on the cake, the extra tiers should be fake since no one will eat those anyway."

. . . that as contemporary weddings become more personal, only family and very close friends receive invitations."

. . . that the IRS frowns on more than five business associates being invited. The IRS considers the wedding a gift, so guests may have to claim food and drink as income and we would have to give them a 1099. It would really embarrass us if we had to ask our friends to put their social security numbers in the guest book." (Forget things like this if your wife or daughter is a CPA.)

Following are some "I read somewhere . . ." blanks for your own use. Whatever you see taking place that can possibly save some money, just write it in. Then you can truthfully say, "I read somewhere. . . ."

"I read somewhere_____."

"I read somewhere_____."

"I read somewhere_____."

Seven

Note missing page numbers in this chapter.

*O*nly one statement has greater power of legitimacy than "I read somewhere . . .," and that's
"I read in **two** different places. . . ." Synergy, what you
have here, says one plus one equals more than two.
The impact of saying you read something in two
places equals a double whammy plus some.

Since the pages don't have numbers, when asked,
"Where did you read it?" you can truthfully say, "I
don't know *exactly*, but I read it in *two* different
places." If you put the old body english on "exactly"
and "two," as in, "I don't know *exactly*, but I read it
in *two* different places," you may see some exciting
things happen. Another statement to add a little

more legitimacy is "If I see it again, I'll show you." You only plan to read the book once, so here again you tell the truth, with the opposing side satisfied that you do have a "legitimate" point.

To make sure you don't get snared in a little fib, it may be helpful to read the list again. Speed-reading encouraged:

"I read somewhere . . .

. . . that it's appropriate for the groom to pick up half the cost of the reception." . . . it's really special to use your grandmother's, mother's, sister's, aunt's, best friend's, casual friend's cake knife." . . . that because of all the sugar brides are getting away from big cakes." . . . the appropriate size and number of flower arrangements at the church is one arrangement in a 1' to 2' vase." . . . it's fashionable to use the flowers from the church at the reception." . . . that all fathers of the bride feel this way." . . . that some misguided people don't like to go to weddings." . . . the local super market was voted #1 in the state for wedding cakes." . . . it is appropriate to have a cash bar." . . . because of people driving afterwards, we should have the bar open for only one hour, or serve only beer and wine, or no bar at all." . . . that because of the high cost of gasoline, modern brides are getting away from limousines." . . . that the best time of day for a wedding is _____." . . . there's a big football game in town that weekend. Parking will be a hassle and hotel space will be hard to come by." . . . that meatballs are people's favorite." . . . it is sentimental and widely accepted that you wear the wedding dress of your mother, sister, aunt, best friend, or casual friend." . . . it's bad luck for the father of the bride to attend a bridal showcase." . . . it is appropriate to share the floral expense with the wedding that takes place before and after yours." . . . really smart, cost-conscious brides are renting their _____." . . . that you should not bring shrimp in from out of state." . . . that you should have only one seafood and one beef." . . . that you should not have seafood and beef together." . . . that flowers from a foreign country sometimes get held up in customs." . . . that the practical, wise bride has the wedding in her home town." . . . that smart brides are renting their wedding dress." . . . that artificial flowers help the environment." . . . that wedding guests dance more and have more fun when fewer tables and chairs are available." . . . that if you have more than three tiers on the cake, the extra tiers should be fake since no one will eat those anyway." . . . that contemporary weddings are becoming more personal, and that only family and very close friends are invited." . . . that the IRS frowns on more than five business associates being invited. The IRS considers the wedding a gift, so guests may have to claim food and drink as income and we would have to give them a 1099. It would really embarrass us if we had to ask our friends to put their social security number in the guest book."

And in case you need to write in your own:

"I read somewhere_____."

"I read somewhere_____."

"I read somewhere_____."

Eight

*I*f you drink adult beverages I suggest you pour a double before you get into this. If you don't drink adult beverages you should seriously consider starting, as it may help you. You can always quit after the wedding and before you go to the judge declaring Chapter 7.

LET'S HAVE A LITTLE HEART-TO-HEART ABOUT THE CAKE!

I don't know much about this cake business, but it definitely looms as one of those boat/airplane deals. I never knew it produced such emotion, especially considering the fact that I have eaten at least one hundred pieces of wedding cake. About ninety-eight of them tasted like old cardboard coated with some of that crumbly sugary stuff they used to print your name on top of the cupcakes when you won the third grade spelling bee.

"Cake-talk" began about halfway through the gestation period in our daughter's engagement. The gestation period for us consumed about a year . . . way too long! The longer the gestation period the more time they have to inflict major financial havoc and for the Hassle Factor Index to exert itself. The ideal scenario for your daughter: meet Mr. Wonderful in September (probably at a football game, which they soon forget), get engaged in October, and marry in November. With quality caterers jammed, good bands and reception places booked, and the wedding gown definitely "off the rack," they run out of time attempting to devastate your dinero.

Anyway, about the midway point I heard "cake-talk." My Hassle Factor Index started quivering when I overheard terms like "on 2 x 4's," "refrigerated truck," "steel rods," and "four-people-six-days." I heard less "construction talk" when we added a room onto our house!

Shortly after my first earful of cake terms my wife and daughter took off to Charlotte, North Carolina (two hundred miles round trip and including lunch, "OF COURSE NOT!" an expense of the wedding), in search of a veil. It appeared that an acceptable veil did not exist anywhere closer than Charlotte, the newly appointed veil capital of the world. Alone, I was reconnoitering the delicatessen section of a really nice supermarket in our neighborhood—my third day without real food, since the furthest thing from their minds before they left was the care and feeding of the breadwinner (no pun intended), and I'm maxed out on apples, grapes, plastic-wrapped cheese, crackers, and bottled water. Even my two black Labs were ticked (no pun intended) because we had run out of their favorite canned food, Chicken à la Lamb, and cut back to that "three dollars per boat load" dry stuff. As the President said during the last oil crisis, "Everyone has to give."

With the banter about the cake fresh on my mind, in this supermarket I happened to walk by the bakery section. Lo and behold I saw something almost incomprehensible—a magnificent, beautifully decorated, four-tiered chocolate butter cream cake. With space between each tier for fresh flowers, it had huge vine-ripened California strawberries and kiwis, white chocolate rosettes, and marzipan grapes, and the entire engineering feat was ringed with edible silver and gold leaves.

I talked to the assistant pastry manager, first shift, and she explained in great detail about the different ingredients and how each layer was made separately. She praised Hans, the pastry chef on second shift, who takes great pride in his work, a real piece of art topped by a lifelike plastic bride and groom—truly a masterpiece fit for a princess, my daughter. I was working up to asking how much it cost when a free sample won me over. It tasted like Grand Marnier-dipped manna from heaven, light-years ahead of any other cake on this nuptial-obsessed planet. If somebody threatened to pound it in your face, you would respond enthusiastically, "Go ahead, take your best shot!"

Excited, I could hardly wait for my wife and daughter to return from Veil Central. Although up to this point I was zero forever in getting ideas accepted by the opposing side, I now had some information of value that I could contribute to the effort, and I finally felt like a key player on the home team.

After I made my carefully rehearsed presentation with childlike enthusiasm, you would have thought I had just told them our cat had died! Neither said a word, not one. The two of them just stared at me—motionless, expressionless, not even blinking their steely eyes, jaws tightly drawn, and hands clasped behind their backs. Surreal. Lights on but nobody home. At that moment, had I wanted to get my beer real cold, I could have placed it next to my wife's heart.

It may have been at that moment, 6:14 P.M. on a rainy, overcast Wednesday three days before Bastille Day, when I crossed that great divide. I stopped living in denial and suddenly came to the cold realization that I really didn't count, that my ideas were not only insane but totally unwelcomed. In that wedding millisecond I came to understand that my role in the whole affair resembled a Brinks' truck driver: Go to the bank with little cap and badge on, load the truck with *all* my money, bring it home, deposit it at their feet, and then excuse myself without a word to return to a life of loneliness and obscurity. Message: I should not be seen or heard from again until thirty seconds before the wedding march begins.

This message gave me an epiphany of only slightly less magnitude than the Hassle Factor Index. They looked at me curiously as I stared off into space, smiling serenely, as a chemical reaction in my brain caused me to think, "I gotta write a book on this! I have a story unfolding before my very eyes that can have tremendous impact on that legion of brothers known as fathers of the bride. All my life, or at least the last year or so, I have wanted to do something that would make a significant difference. Carpe Diem! I may receive an honorary degree from a major university for this body of work that enables men everywhere to better understand the opposing side. Maybe, just maybe, in their darkest hours, my words of wisdom will keep the lines of the Hassle Factor Index from snuffing out fraternal lives. Even if a father of a bride has to declare personal bankruptcy because of his daughter's wedding, hope triumphs with the help of a book and the award-winning KWOMS Society."

My advice on the wedding cake went down like the experience of the Jewish businessman in Jerusalem who went to the Wailing Wall every day and earnestly prayed for several hours. An elderly shopkeeper nearby, a compassionate and observant woman, saw him every morning for six months perform this ritual at the Wall. Always alone, he did not appear a happy man. In her concern one day she approached the man as he finished his prayers. When asked if she could help, he said no, that he had great concern about his wife and daughter. His daughter was getting married in a few months, and since the engagement they had argued incessantly with each other, business was bad, and they had spent lots of money he did not have. He told her that this whole wedding affair had hurt his family in many ways and that he sought divine guidance. The shopkeeper asked if he thought the prayer did any good, and he replied forlornly, "It's like I'm talking to a wall."

Needless to say, my opposing side went to a wedding cake "artist" in Charleston—Ava from Sweden (several trips on this item which "OF COURSE NOT!" came from the wedding budget). I never asked what it cost, a classic case of "don't ask, don't tell."

$$ $$$

Cakes can be priced anywhere from fifty dollars to, grab your dough (no pun intended), several thousand! All I know is that something appears out of whack when one piece of cake costs as much as dinner at a Five Star restaurant.

If your daughter abstains from physical fitness, she will change her mind about a month before the wedding. She and her Mom will mosey on down to the gym, talk them into a one-month special membership with personal trainer, which "OF COURSE NOT!" counts as an expense of the wedding. They start working out, pumping iron and crunching like never before . . . and never again!

This might be the perfect time to try, "I read somewhere that because of the high sugar and fat content, total cholesterol, high sodium, deathly amounts of carbohydrates, and an average of two million calories, health-conscious brides get away from big cakes, substituting fat-free yogurt with fresh blueberries!" Say it with enthusiasm as if your retirement savings depend on it, because it does!

Don't put too much hope in this since KWOMS Society research shows the chance of the opposing side not having a cake falls to a diminutive 0.1 on the WPS. When Marie Antoinette said, "Let them eat cake," obviously she'd never had a daughter get married!

Nine

*O*ne of the most interesting concepts I've used in my work is based on the fact that each person, born with a certain behavioral style, or personality, has a unique identity. I developed a self-scored instrument called the F.A.C.E. of Leadership™, which enables people to discover their own unique styles and shows them how to blend those styles with others to have more productive relationships.

An overview of these styles will help you understand and predict the behavior of the opposing side during the gestation period. But beware: Totally understanding and predicting behavior of the opposing side as the wedding draws closer and jaws of the Hassle Factor Index begin to close grades out a rock solid 0.0 on the WPS—about as easy as shooting a bat with a bow and arrow!

Each person falls into one or more of four different styles, very easy to remember with the acronym **F.A.C.E.**

**Forceful
Analytical
Cooperative
Enthusiastic**

You have *some* of each trait. How much you have of each and in what combination determines your behavioral style. Look at the following four columns of words (a shortened version of the longer, more involved instrument) and pick the whole column of words most descriptive of you. If two columns describe you equally, then pick two columns.

Results-Oriented	Systematic	Patient	Carefree
Domineering	Neat	Low-Key	Sociable
Demanding	Accurate	Predictable	Optimistic
Impatient	Likes Facts	Steady	Outgoing
Strong Willed	Likes Order	Team Player	Impulsive
Direct	Thorough	Helpful	Persuasive
Bottom-Line	Perfectionist	Not Hurried	Positive
Assertive	Evaluates	Sincere	People-Oriented
Daring	Meticulous	Gets Along	Promoter
Decisive	Critical	Loyal	Talker
Competitive	Seeks Quality	Listener	Disorganized
Hurried	High Standards	Family-Oriented	Spontaneous
Risk Taker	Concentrates	Willing	Entertains

The first column describes the Forceful style, second column Analytical, third column Cooperative, and fourth column Enthusiastic. The one you picked represents your primary behavioral style. If you picked only one of the four, then pick the next one that most accurately describes you. This represents your secondary style. Most individuals either have two that describe them equally or one high and one slightly less.

A description of the four styles follows. Read all four with particular emphasis on the ones you picked for yourself, then we will explore what tendencies you can expect from the opposing side during the gestation period.

FORCEFUL

These people take authority, make quick decisions, like to solve problems, want immediate results through rapid action, see trouble as simply a challenge to reach their goals, and constantly question the status quo. Seeking direct answers, power, and prestige from individual accomplishments, they don't like being controlled or supervised. They like change, get bored unless faced with various new activities, and constantly seek ways to advance their careers. Forcefuls want to control their environment and overcome opposition.

ANALYTICAL

Perfectionists, critical thinkers, and detail-oriented, they double-dot the i's and triple-cross the t's. Although diplomatic, they sometimes criticize others. They follow procedures to the letter, constantly seek quality by accurately adhering to high standards, don't like unannounced changes, and are inherently slow in making decisions. They seek security, reassurance, and recognition of their efforts. Analyticals excel as planners but need precise descriptions of desired results.

COOPERATIVE

Patient, loyal, good listeners, these people are a calming influence, are sincere, and identify readily with a group. Family-oriented and "traditional," they seek to maintain the status quo and value security. Able to develop special skills and concentrate on the job at hand, they want credit for their efforts, obey the rules, seek out and follow procedures, and are team-oriented. Cooperatives work best with sincere individuals capable and willing to praise them for their contributions.

ENTHUSIASTIC

Team-oriented "people people," Enthusiastics like making a good impression, talking, entertaining, and encouraging enthusiasm. They want to help others, interact in a group, create a motivated work force, and seek popularity, recognition of accomplishments, and good relationships. They like to coach, counsel, express themselves openly, and join group activities, especially those that bring social recognition. Enthusiastics dislike details and being controlled, and they have trouble staying on task.

The above describe people and their "normal" behavior. Of course during the gestation period, with Hysteriamones running wild, we cease to deal with "normal" behavior, so you can expect the opposing side to operate thusly:

FORCEFUL

Forcefuls, sometimes called "Wedding Nazis," want to make quick decisions on the place, cake, dress, menu, and flowers. Since they have the patience of a pit bull on steroids, they do not like to shop around. If they see something they like and the price seems reasonable, they buy it on the spot: "Wrap it up, let's go!"

If the church says you can't have a rock band, the Forcefuls want to know who made such a stupid rule and demand a meeting with the Pope to get the rule changed. If that doesn't work, they proceed with the band anyway, figuring that it's "easier to ask for forgiveness than permission." If experiencing a long gestation period, they get bored with the whole process and suggest that eloping or getting a mail order groom from Russia would make life easier.

They like the "no-huddle" approach, and if things go too smoothly they call an audible at the last minute to inject a little excitement back into the game. Forcefuls hate and prefer to delegate most of the details, the ones they save for themselves forgotten on game day. They demand a ceremony no more than seven minutes long and think this whole wedding deal could cosummate more efficiently over the Internet. They have big egos, and if somebody tells them they did a good job on the wedding, they respond, "I know it." They see themselves as benevolent dictators and captains of "The Good Ship Wedding."

ANALYTICAL

Analyticals drive you nuts from day one of the gestation period because they obsess about details, even on the details that don't matter, for instance making sure six *live* petals exist on each flower. They will chase a nickel in a checkbook for six months and want to know *everything*, and everything must be perfect—perfect lighting, perfect flowers, perfect dress, and most of all perfect groom. They get supercritical of others for being two minutes late and refuse to delegate, convinced that if the wedding needs organization they will have to orchestrate it. Even if they go over budget (Hysteriamones 1 and 2 are powerful stuff and override certain behavioral tendencies), they know exactly where the dollars went. Analyticals have every receipt, phone call, and VISA charge on Excel, updated hourly, one file away from the 175-item wedding checklist, which takes up two full megabytes of memory. Analyticals want the ceremony to be *exactly* one hour, very serious, with thirty minutes of instruction from the minister on how the young couple should run their lives . . . which *they* have written!

COOPERATIVE

Cooperative types personify teamwork as they try to make sure everybody gets along through the entire process (twenty-seven pictures of the family in their wallets), their big fear being that the family starts bickering. They listen to suggestions and won't get all bent out of shape when something goes wrong, which of course happens—a perfect 10 on the WPS. They simply repair it and move on. However, they don't like surprises except on Christmas morning. If the bride and mother of the bride fit the Cooperative mold, fortune smiles with smooth sailing in the forecast. The chance of both of them being the Cooperative type grades out about 1.2 on the WPS.

ENTHUSIASTIC

Enthusiastics want lots of people there whether they know them or not. To them a wedding is not a religious experience, but simply the opportunity to put on one heck of a great party at someone else's expense, meaning yours. Very emotional, they laugh or cry at the drop of a veil, and they do the dropping. They want a team effort and a *big* team. A loud, at minimum ten-piece band performs among tons of bright, multicolored flowers, a dozen ice carvings, and a cake big enough to feed the Second Marine Division. The number of bridesmaids equals the number of people standing in line at the DMV on the last day of the month. Their jewelry will set off the airport metal detector from the curb. Sunshine is their favorite color.

When the critiques come in they want everyone to boast of the greatest extravaganza ever. Disorganized, but unlike the Forcefuls who will delegate the details, Enthusiastics have no clue about details. When the checkbook gets out of balance they just change banks. For them the traffic light of spending is stuck on bright green. Always running late, the whole afternoon of the wedding will be shot doing hair, make-up, facials, massages, pedicures, and manicures because it is of utmost importance that they look good. They call the caterer, get a wrong number, invite a stranger to the wedding and make a friend for life! Their ideal ceremony: forty-five minutes, forty minutes of which is popular music with a guitar, violin, and snare drum.

I trust you see the problem here. Depending on the behavioral style of the opposing side, life offers many difficulties during the gestation period. What do you think would happen if the mother of the bride *and* the bride surface as Forcefuls—stand by for a battle! What if they both emerge as Enthusiastics— a great party for sure but an organizational nightmare saved only by the hiring of a competent, highly Analytical wedding coordinator. What if the mother of the bride combines high Forceful and high Analytical?—this is a tough one because she wants everything done *right* now her way *and* done perfectly. How about this combination: Analytical mother and Enthusiastic daughter? They will drive each other crazy!

Be aware of what happens when the jaws of the Hassle Factor Index begin to close and the pressure gets intense. My good friend Al Walker refers to this as Z'ing. The Enthusiastic may take on some tendencies of the Analytical, the Analytical may become more like a Cooperative, and the Cooperative may behave like an Enthusiastic. Under mild pressure the Forcefuls become . . . well, more Forceful!

To a small degree the opposing side actually changes behavior style. You may think they have lost their minds and morphed into strange creatures. Don't worry about this natural phenomenon; as soon as the bride and groom say "I do," everyone returns to normal.

$ $$ $$$

Forcefuls will not be taken advantage of on money, but their lack of patience prevents them from shopping around for good deals and they pay more "just to get it done."

The Analyticals help out because they look for good value, shop around, and make decisions based on facts, not emotions.

Cooperatives contribute optimism because of their conservative nature. However, they cave in sometimes on money just to keep the peace.

For Enthusiastics you need to put your bank account on death watch, as they want an awe-inspiring, dynamite, majestic, opulent, and knock-your-socks-off Mardi Gras festival (they stopped calling it a wedding a long time ago). They make spending decisions totally on emotion without regard to cost. Their mantra: "Figure out how to pay for it later."

WARNING

It makes no difference how the opposing side was hard-wired on day one. Just remember that the magic potion Hysteriamone always tries to turn the opposing side into a dangerous alloy of creativity and spending. When the bouquet hits the air you will need the Hubble Telescope and a GPS to locate your net worth!

Ten

My son, Jake, graduated from the College of Charleston in Charleston, South Carolina. My daughter also graduated from the College of Charleston. My wife grew up in Charleston. My daughter met her husband in Charleston. They all *love* Charleston. You probably have guessed where this leads: They wanted a Charleston wedding, and since *they* all wanted it, guess what?—a Charleston wedding, just about a 240-mile round trip from our home in Columbia to the beautiful Trinity United Methodist Church on Meeting Street. I have no explanation why we didn't *move* to Charleston thousands of dollars ago—I could make the drive in my sleep!

Don't get me wrong, Charleston is a great city. If you have never been there, I highly recommend a visit. It has a lot to offer: beautiful beaches, golf (Kiawah Island and the Ocean Course where they played the Ryder Cup is magnificent), sailing, deep sea fishing, antebellum homes, out-of-this-world restaurants (especially seafood), and digging into the history would keep Shelby Foote occupied for years (Fort Sumter, where the Civil War started, can be seen from downtown). So come on down, bring a lot of money and leave it; we thank you in advance! However, I hesitate recommending Charleston for a wedding because it abuses the privilege of being "pricey." Also, you might want to visit in the spring or fall as the summer months are a little hot and humid. We had Allison's wedding in early November, a perfect time weatherwise.

Back to business. Discourage at all costs whatever you hear about having the wedding "out of town." The term "destination wedding" refers to the large chunk of your money that goes to the "destination." Mileage, hotel, long distance charges, meals, parking, and no telling what else does you in, and all this just in *preparation* for the wedding. And *all* of these expenses ahead of time "OF COURSE NOT!" come from the wedding budget.

If you have an out-of-town wedding, you come out better by bolting an ATM machine in the back of your wife's SUV and renting the opposing side an apartment there for the last six months of the gestation period. Maybe they will eat a meal or two in and save you some jack (1.6 on the WPS).

When Jake graduated he went to Jackson Hole, Wyoming, to be a ski bum. He worked in restaurants and, in his own words, lived in "poverty with a view!" I caused one of the saddest faces ever when I had to tell my only son, "You know I planned to help you with your trip out west, help you trade in the 1987 Honda with 173,000 miles, broken air conditioner, no muffler, and driver's side window that won't open. I intended to help you with a deposit on an apartment in Jackson Hole. Well, Jake, after your sister's wedding I can't afford to help you. And by the way, can you loan me five dollars for lunch?"

While in college one of his favorite pastimes was shrimping with his buddies in the creeks along the coast around Charleston. According to Jake's recipe they made up a meal of half clay and half fishmeal, added water, patted it into a ball about the size of a navel orange, threw it into the creek, and the shrimp would immediately go into a feeding frenzy. They would cast their net, pull it in, and voila! . . . fresh shrimp for the barbie!

Exactly the same thing happens at an event known as the Bridal Showcase. The wedding vendors get a "meal" together of wedding "stuff"—gowns, veils, shoes, invitations, bands, cakes, photography, travel, ice sculptures, tuxedos, flowers, and caterers. They invite about a thousand brides-to-be who, just like the shrimp, go into a feeding frenzy. The vendors cast

their nets, and voila! . . . fresh shrimp for the barbie—the ultimate target-rich environment for wedding vendors.

During our gestation period I was never invited
by the opposing side to go to a Bridal Showcase, and
I am not even sure whether or not they went to one.
I do remember a trip they made to Atlanta (400-mile
round trip that "OF COURSE NOT!" counts as an
expense of the wedding). I suspect, with the secrecy
surrounding this trip, either they went to a Bridal
Showcase or they masquerade as CIA operatives.

While doing research for this book (not a whole lot
of research, mind you, just reporting observations), I
actually went to a Bridal Showcase to see this phenomenon in action. Astounding, especially the number of people there. No wonder weddings rack up
$32 billion a year. There were over one hundred
booths set up for vendors. On the other end of the
vendors away from the registration table, strategic-
ally placed so the future brides had to walk the
gauntlet of vendors, a stage held a fashion show that
lasted for three hours. Needless to say, it took about
thirty seconds of this Gown-A-Rama to see and hear
all I wanted to know about tuxedos and bridal wear.

On a rather cold and rainy Sunday afternoon in
January, while the first round of NFL playoffs was
under way, on a perfect day for watching football, I
went to the Showcase between games and was blown
away by the number of young men, prospective
grooms, attending. While I didn't do any interviews to

determine their motivation for being there, I can only guess three possible reasons:

1. Generation X or Y (haven't quite got the ages of these generations figured out) young men seem more involved in things like this than you and I at that age. All in all I think this bodes well—a little odd but good.

2. The prospective grooms may have been there to protect their own financial interests. Possibly in a moment of TRI (Temporary Romantical Insanity), they agreed to pick up the tab for something that some scrooge Dad would not. Of course, this would have been something *really* important, like a hand-carved ice sculpture of the grammar school where the bride and groom first met.

3. The last possible reason for the prospective grooms being there: They, like most of us in the courtship scenario, agreed to do something like this just because their true love asked them. At the same time they put Bridal Showcase on the top of the list, presented the day after the wedding, of things they *never* ever agree to do again in their lifetime. Other things on the list:

Ballroom dancing lessons
Christmas shopping in the mall

Miss any of the following:
  Final round of the Masters
  Super Bowl
  Daytona 500
  Seventh game of the World Series
  Final Four
  Opening of any season (duck, fish,
    deer, dove, turkey, etc.)
Show wedding photos to guy friends
Go to a ballet
Attend the wedding of someone
  he doesn't know
Decorate the Christmas tree
Clean up after the bride's dog
Wear a tuxedo again
And the list goes on!

Two other things caught my attention. First, as far as I could tell, not a single other Dad was in attendance, and I promise the crowd numbered at least a thousand. Go figure. Second, the prospective grooms didn't look too happy. As a matter of fact most of them looked absolutely miserable, which confirms my suspicion that reason number three may have been the motivation for most.

While flying with the Reserves we had drill one weekend a month, although getting our flying minimums took an average of five or six additional days each month. Drill, usually on a different weekend each time—probably to confuse the Russians—was always a command performance unless you had a date with Miss America, tickets to the Super Bowl, or it was the opening of dove season. These events qualified as "significant personal learning opportunities." The airline guys always played the patriotic card and claimed "national economic necessity" when they needed to miss drill, a little BS the heavies never did figure out. Since nobody knew, including my family, exactly which weekend drill fell on, whenever something I wanted to miss came up, all I had to say was, "I have drill that weekend; my country needs me." No one ever questioned it. Now that I think about it, I should never have let it be known that I retired. I could still be saying, "I have drill that weekend."

I wouldn't suggest joining the Reserves to get out of a Bridal Showcase, but it might be smart to have one good excuse for this one tucked away, kinda like the trick play a football team uses in the fourth quarter when they gotta have a first down. Just trust me, you don't want to go to a Bridal Showcase. You might try, "I read somewhere that it's bad luck for a father of the bride to attend a Bridal Showcase." Or fake a heart attack, because if you go, it might give you one!

$ $$$

Whether it's a good idea or not for the opposing side to go to a Bridal Showcase depends on where they fall on the spending curve. If they, overall, hold the $ mindset, you should discourage them from going, because I guarantee they will hit upon a bumpercrop of ideas that require more money as they try to upgrade all the essential and nonessential elements.

If they break the bank on the third level of cost overruns (8.8 on the WPS), it might be a good idea for them to go because they might find some way, as a random act of guilt kicks in, to save some money (1.1 on the WPS).

It may be a bit charitable to say they will *save* you money. They may save money in one area, but you can lay odds they already have that money spent in another area—a classic **Zero Sum Game**!

> *It's all a game and the sum of it is that you will have zero when it's over.*

In the history of weddingdom there has ***never*** been any money left over. Think federal debt and you have the picture!

Eleven

*A*nother great trial and tribulation is who to invite —or interestingly, who *not* to invite. In fact this may be the biggest ordeal you undergo, short of bankruptcy.

Of course if money is not an object, as the opposing side thinks, you can get out your Rolodex, PDA, phone book, church roster, Chamber of Commerce directory, and old college annual and invite every single person whose name sounds even slightly familiar. This includes heads of state, politicians, movie stars, and Randy, the waiter at the restaurant the other night. You don't know his last name? That's OK, the opposing side will find out!

KWOMS

You will hear the opposing side say "We *have* to invite" him, her, or them because:

1. "They saw Margaret [the bride] in the ballet."
2. "We saw them in the mall when Margaret turned two, and they said how cute she was."
3. "She invited us to a Tupperware party twelve years ago."
4. "Her second cousin by a third marriage wed our great aunt's niece's half sister who babysat Margaret once when we went to see Reba McEntire at The Pavilion, where we sat next to Jan . . . oh my goodness, we almost forgot Jan!"
5. "I just know they will invite us to their daughter Patricia's wedding" (Patricia is eight years old).
6. "Their daughter Millie befriended Margaret in school." ("School" to the opposing side covers *all* schooling starting with day one of first grade.) In this case Millie, in Margaret's first grade class for two weeks, came over to the house once for cookies and milk. Her father, an on-again, off-again welder, machinist, engineer, inventor, and tinkerer, and his yoga-instructor wife took a job in Yakima, Washington, designing car-top ski racks. Margaret and Millie stumbled across each other in an Internet chat room on private jet charters to exotic honeymoon destinations.

7. "She was the nurse in the hospital who warm-
ed up Margaret's formula."

If money is not an object and you have managed
to acquire considerable net worth that you don't
mind forfeiting, you have my unqualified admira-
tion. However, like most of us mortals to whom
money *does* count, this issue of "The List," a most
weighty matter, carries a specific gravity similar to
Plutonium.

Think about this for a moment: One stamp on one
invitation, as it runs its course through the whole
process of this wedding juggernaut, could mean
eighty dollars out of your pocket. One stamp! I trust
you grasp the implications of this—ten stamps means
at least ten people, probably more, and could cost you
a minimum of eight hundred dollars! Just three more
—hey, you can do the disheartening math! Serious
stuff here, and let me tell you from personal experience, the opposing side loves nothing more than putting stamps on invitations.

Just picture them in your den, maybe with a few
girlfriends to help (if they need help just putting
stamps on, you can skip the idea of a financial rainy
day; this describes a Noah and the Ark flood type of
day, a forty days and forty nights orgy of spending).
There they sit, sipping Kendall Jackson Chardonnay
and munching on catered stuffed mushrooms and
marinated shrimp, all of which "OF COURSE NOT!"
is part of the wedding budget. You serve the role of
the indispensable but invisible wine steward.

You watch in bewilderment at the sea of invitations, wave upon wave like the North Shore of Oahu in the winter with the big ones coming in. They move with assembly-line precision around the portable Ping-Pong table, covered with resplendent silk tablecloths that have transformed the family entertainment piece into the "shrine of betrothal."

You scrutinize for the first time the elegantly engraved, die-cut, Pantone matched copper ink invitation on 37.5 lb. gilt-edged vellum paper. It has double embassy envelopes, the inside one black satin moiré lined, the outside blind embossed with sealing wax. You will find out later that the stranger with the French beret, batik shirt, rope belt, sandals, dark glasses, and Shih Tzus is a professional calligrapher, an expert in the Open Antique Roman font.

You know they could have gotten plain printing ($) for a fraction of the cost, or even raised printing, known as thermography ($$) and practically indistinguishable from engraving, for a whole lot less. Oh no, we fly first class ($$$) on this, the tip of the financial spear.

You realize, with cascading tear ducts, palpitating heart, and accelerating Hassle Factor Index, that every flip of their delicate wrists and nimble fingers will cost you eighty bucks . . . or more!

A great money-saving thought comes to mind: You volunteer to mail the invitations. You could, on the way, take the invitations down to your office, stuff them with the flyer announcing the big semiannual-two-for-one-half-off-get-one-free-with-mail-in-rebate-sale, and write the whole thing off as a business expense. Of course this would be viewed as the most rude, crude, and socially unacceptable stunt in the history of weddingdom, and the cost in grief from the opposing side would far outweigh the benefit. Besides, you couldn't run this "brick" through the postage machine anyway.

Some days you are the pigeon.
Some days you are the statue.

When approached thirty minutes after the engagement in a year-long gestation period about whether Sam, a certain business associate, and his wife Carla should be invited, I made perhaps the biggest communication blunder of my life when I innocently responded, "I don't think they would want to come." From the immediate and incredulous double take you would have thought I'd just insulted the Queen. The scowls and howls of indignation that I should even hint that one of our friends would not just die to attend our daughter's nuptial still echo.

Being a Harvard-trained negotiator with lots of practice in the backstroke during thirty years of marriage, I immediately put oars in the suddenly turbulent family waters. While taking a couple of swift pulls and trying to recoup lost ground I apologetically responded, "I didn't mean *I* didn't think they wouldn't want to come. I just read somewhere that some people, maybe just a few, for whatever their misguided reasons, don't like to go to weddings."

I waited an interminable second to see if my quick wits would allow me to escape or that window of opportunity had been slammed shut and I had just bulldozed myself into a pit of recrimination, reprehension, and denunciation. I could see in their steely eyes and body language a flicker of hope that I had escaped unscathed, although I knew if I had, I certainly had expended one more of my nine lives and that, like Shaquille O'Neal with four fouls, a couple more slip-ups and I would be toast.

One of the most beautiful statements I ever heard followed from my wife: "You may be right about some people, but none of *our* friends would feel that way." When they turned and walked away after this too close call, I let out a sigh of relief that almost collapsed my lungs. In that pivotal moment the thought hit me—in the future I would always respond, "I have no *kwoms* about them being invited."

As time went on I noticed something very strange: I actually changed from saying, "I have no *kwoms* about them being invited" to "I have no *qualms* about them being invited" to "They might *like* to come" . . . to finally, "They would *love* to come." I don't know exactly when this transition occurred, but as the gestation period progressed, I started to believe that everyone *does* want to come to our daughter's wedding. It's amazing that if you say or hear "They would love to come" over and over again, you start to believe it—kinda like that baseball movie. You can have moments of delusion during all this.

Somewhere in the deep recesses of my mind a little voice kept popping up, "Don't let them get to you on this, there's too much money at stake. Right, Farrell, everyone does *not* want to go to a wedding." This reassuring voice went a little further, which gave me great inspiration: "It's nothing personal, but contrary to what the opposing side thinks, a *lot* of people just don't like weddings at all, and you would do some of your friends a great favor if you could somehow keep them *off* the list. In fact you have a moral responsibility to do so!" Surely a revelation of cosmic proportions; I could save eighty dollars apiece and make my friends happy at the same time. Wow! Most times when you make friends happy it costs something; you give them a gift, take them to dinner, or give them sports tickets.

But I had a dilemma: On one hand I could almost believe that everyone *does* want to come, while on the other hand my inner voice said, "Not true, don't cave in, keep your head on straight." What to believe, and more important, what to do, especially with this "moral responsibility" intimation? I decided the only way to answer this question was to simply ask the people on the list, "Do you *really* want to come to my daughter's wedding?"

However, there's an obvious problem here: Suppose a friend of yours came to you and asked, "Do you want to come to my daughter's wedding? It's on

KWOMS

Super Bowl Sunday, eighty miles from here on a dirt road somewhere in the boondocks, at the Holy Ecumenical Trinity Reformation Gethsemane Redeemer Church of the Holy United Living Springs. I can't remember what country her fine young man hails from, but their custom requires a long service so eat before you come. It starts at three o'clock and they promise to finish by six, reception in the church social hall with goat's milk and food kin to Greek, but not quite." What's your answer to a good friend?—"Of course, I'd love to." You may have your fingers crossed behind your back, but you can only give that answer to a friend.

So asking people I knew wouldn't work. After much thought the idea finally hit—I would do a survey of the people who attended my seminars. Since I do seminars all over the country, the participants wouldn't even know I had a daughter, much less a wedding coming up.

The men and women I surveyed probably averaged forty years old, most had children, at least half were college graduates, and their jobs ranged from administrative assistant to top-level executives. The groups included engineers, accountants, nurses, athletic directors from major universities, bankers—a real cross section. My seminars, mostly on leadership issues, attract nice folks, but folks who, probably like you, shoot straight and would give honest answers.

I gave them the written survey without offering any reason, my total instructions on the order of, "If you would, please take a minute to fill this out; when done pass them to the front." It took no more than a minute, and after they passed them up I explained it in a fun way, we had a big laugh, and we went on with the seminar.

In the survey I gave to over four hundred people, note that the only demographic information I requested was male or female, which proved very helpful.

SURVEY

Rank in order from 1 (most) to 8 (least) how you would like to spend a Saturday if you could do only one of the following. Read the entire list before ranking.

_____ watch your favorite football team play

_____ go shopping at the mall

_____ walk in the park

_____ attend a wedding

_____ mow the yard

_____ participate in your favorite sport: golf, tennis, hiking, hunting, etc.

_____ weekend trip to the beach

_____ go to a movie

Circle one: female male

Here are the results of the survey:

5.0   watch your favorite football team play
5.1   go shopping at the mall
4.2   walk in the park
6.6   attend a wedding
5.8   mow the yard
3.2   participate in your favorite sport: golf,
       tennis, hiking, hunting, etc.
2.3   weekend trip to the beach
3.9   go to a movie

The second biggest communication mistake I ever made was when I totally disregarded the last two words in this book's title and shared this data with my wife. She immediately shot back, after placing hands on hips, cocking head to one side, and pursing lips, "Well, you worded the survey wrong. You should have said what *two* things would you like to do on a Saturday since you could do something in addition to the wedding [not necessarily true], and you only had one other negative thing, mow the yard [note a little Freudian slip here, one *other* "negative thing"]. And one other shortcoming in your error-filled survey: You should have put on there your best friend's wedding, your niece's or nephew's wedding. Now, please give me that other box of stamps" (note that she didn't say roll!).

I dutifully kept my mouth shut but was thinking, "Look, my name is not Gallup. This has not been done scientifically. Still out there hustling trying to earn enough to pay for this spectacle, I don't have time to put into this. I just ask the questions, you decipher the results." I did mouth the words . . . while she walked away!

Here's how I figure it: Most people—not all, but most people, men and women—don't jump up and down every day just dying to go to a wedding. Men, especially, don't get up on Saturday morning after a big party the night before and say, "Gee, I don't want to watch that playoff game, or play golf, or go out on my boat. What I really want to do on this beautiful Saturday, after working my tail off all week, is get all dressed up, drive one hundred miles round trip, and go to a wedding!" Figures don't lie. Case closed!

A few moments later my wife stormed back in. With wild eyes and nostrils flaring she said, "And one more thing [of course it's *never* just *one* more thing when it concerns the wedding]! Your results are all skewed up [clever play on words; I'll claim those as my own]. You figured the men in with the women and anybody with half a brain knows that men, especially *your* football-watching, golf-addicted, duck-hunting, bass-fishing, jet-flying, NASCAR-chasing, spitting, and crotch-scratching friends [see chapter 9 on personality changes] probably scored weddings last, which means most of the intelligent, mature, and caring women just love weddings!" [Read this last part again with the emphasis on **love** and you'll get a feel for her disposition at the time.]   .

Too late now, having passed the point of no return, I had been challenged and backed into a competitive corner. This had turned into a battle of wills, and I would not be denied this moment to prove my point. Figures don't lie and I just knew they were on my side.

So I revisited the survey results, as if I had nothing else to do with my life, and refigured men vs. women. My wife guessed right in that the men scored weddings lower than the women did, but not by a whole lot. Also note the two things women scored lower than men do! More about these two later. The results:

Men	Women	
3.9	6.1	watch your favorite football team play
6.0	4.2	go shopping at the mall
4.6	3.8	walk in the park
7.2	**6.0**	**attend a wedding**
5.2	6.3	mow the yard
2.2	4.2	participate in your favorite sport: golf, tennis, hiking, hunting, etc.
2.8	1.8	weekend trip to the beach
4.1	3.6	go to a movie

I couldn't wait to give this proof to the opposing side and glow in the knowledge that at least on one point with this wedding business I was right and they were wrong. But my inner voice spoke up again:

"Don't do it, Farrell. Just a skirmish in the big war, don't put what precious little credibility you have on the line with bigger fish to catch, bigger money to save." I heeded my own advice and slinked back to my office to labor in obscurity, knowing this subject should not be broached again.

Although I have always believed in never letting the truth stand in the way of a good story, I did in fact do the survey and these are the real results. And as a bonus there may be something else to learn here.

Math was easy for me until about the sixth grade when x's and y's were introduced. I immediately fell behind the power curve and never recovered. In college statistics I was really on the dark side of the moon. Thank goodness for Dr. Tomlin, Patron Saint of Seniors, who would never flunk a senior in statistics. When the professor talked about Euclidean distance, Cronbach's Alpha coefficient, algorithms and cluster analysis, he might as well have been talking about nuclear fusion or explaining Hawking's Black Hole Theory.

While I don't have a clue how to interpret all this earth-shattering data from a statistical point of view (and by the way, the fact that not a single social scientist has offered me any money for this extensive and time-consuming research does not necessarily indicate its value), after studying this data for oh, about ninety seconds, I have drawn some conclusions that could benefit you as father of the bride.

1. If your wife gets really torqued at you about this wedding stuff, which will happen (9.4 on the WPS), the data shows that the best way to smooth it over is to invite her for a weekend at the beach. Here's the rub: If you live along the coast, say in Jacksonville, Florida; Corpus Christi, Texas; Virginia Beach, Virginia; Corona del Mar or San Francisco, California, you have it wired. Jump in the car about noon, run out to the beach, enjoy a picnic, smooth things over, and drive back in time to catch the last few holes of The Masters. If, however, your zip code is in Kansas City, Denver, Sioux Falls, or Albuquerque, you have a serious problem because when they say "beach," they ain't talking about the public boat ramp beach at the Lake of the Ozarks. They mean "**The Beach**," as in Atlantic, Pacific, Gulf of Mexico. I guess it all depends on the depth of the boiling cauldron in which you swim. One thing for sure: Don't make the offer if unwilling to deliver the goods.

2. When in trouble, don't ever ask, "What can I do to make it up to you?" This, a dangerously worded closed-end question, may elicit, "Take me to the beach." You would be smart to pick a couple of the top four you can afford and say, "I'm real sorry, dear, let me make it up to you. Would you like to go for a walk,

or go to a movie?" (For goodness sakes let her pick the movie! Don't suggest *Terminator II*!)

WARNING * WARNING * WARNING

Ignoring this warning could get you severely beaten about the head and shoulders.

3. Explicit data shows that when your wife gets really PO'd at you, don't ever, ever, ever, ever ask, "Would you like to watch a football game with me?" Now you and I know a sincere invitation like this shows a great deal of love and respect—your willingness to share an important moment like the NFC Championship with your wife. For some strange reason wives don't see it this way. In fact, it has been shown that if you make the offer it may and probably will worsen the situation. Forget football unless your wife wears one of those cheesehead things every Sunday during football season.

4. As the gestation period goes along and the lines in the Hassle Factor Index begin to move inevitably toward one another, your wife may come under a certain amount of stress (9.2 on the WPS). Numbers again tell us that you do not *ever* want to say something like, "Dear, you look a little frazzled and appear as if you need some exercise. Why don't you go out

and mow the yard . . . and be careful around the petunias." Saying this would not be wise, especially if you are in your leather recliner watching ESPN, popping a cool one with chip and dip at the ready!

$$\mathbf{\$\$\$}$$

You may not grasp the seriousness of this invitation business until you get to the chapter on receptions. However, do not dip your toe into the chilly reception waters of chapter 14 as you probably need more time to mentally prepare for the leap. Just remember, if you can get it across to the other side (1.8 on the WPS), you will not hurt many feelings if you keep a friend off the list, and in fact you may pick up a lifelong debt of gratitude if you do! Remember, "I read somewhere. . . ."

✳ ✳ ✳ ✳

One more thought: Why would we invite someone we really don't want to invite to the wedding, and why would that person come to the wedding when he or she would really rather not? It's a real paradox—in fact, it could almost be called an *Abilene Paradox*. If you have never read *The Abilene Paradox*, it can be found at the end of this book.

Twelve

Where there's confusion there's profit.

Nothing in the wedding world causes more confusion than flowers—and it's painfully obvious who gets confused and who makes the profit.

Breakaway, pave style, cascade, pomander, bimah, hoop, ikebana, nosegay, crescent, air dry, freeze dry, circlet, fish bowls, biedermeier, garland, bouquet, topiaries, dessicants, boutonniere, and *tussy mussy* (no joke on this last one).

What in the name of Martha Stewart goes on here? Give *me* a break! KWOMS Society research shows that men, on average, have *heard* of only three of the above in their lifetime and can accurately describe only one, that being boutonniere. At their senior proms several decades ago their dates gave them white carnations from the neighborhood grocery store coolers. Each flower was pinned, "on the *left* side, you culturally challenged cretin." And it was the first thing tossed out the window after a date was delivered back home—have you *ever* seen a white carnation on a guy's bulletin board? If you have, he is automatically and permanently blackballed as a potential member of the KWOMS Society!

Here's the problem for you as the opposing side lays siege to your castle: KWOMS Society research shows that 87 percent of women don't know any more than men about this "floral" stuff. So when they go shopping for flowers, like men going shopping for a bulldozer, they haven't had a whole lot of experience. As a result they just might end up buying the whole nursery and you'll have to weed-eat your way out of the church.

Of course, that's life—the opposing side will be real experienced in weddings—after the wedding is over! Just like a parachute—if not there the first time you need it, you probably won't need it again! This "wedding experience" comes in handy only if you have another daughter or two coming along later. In this case you have my sincere condolences in advance!

It may be somewhat cathartic for me to share with you a bad flashback I experience every time I think of flowers in relation to a wedding. Maybe by confessing I can finally exorcise some financial demons that have tortured me for a while.

One evening prior to our daughter's nuptials my wife and I started discussing flowers. Actually, my wife discussed; I just kept saying, "I have no *kwoms* about topiaries. I have no *kwoms* about desiccants. I have no *kwoms* about pomander" (as if I had a clue what she talked about). The wedding, two weeks away, had reached critical mass and was moving forward at full throttle. The war had been lost, and I, the Dad, was just hanging on for dear life, trying to stop the jaws of the Hassle Factor Index from smashing me like a laser-guided smart bomb.

The phone rang, late (not a good sign). It was Allison, almost hysterical (pun intended) as she exclaimed between sobs, "Mark fell . . . off . . . his roof. He . . . broke . . . his ankle and . . . may have . . . other injuries. Should . . . we . . . postpone . . . the wedding?"

Within one wedding millisecond a lump the size of Maine formed in my throat, my blood pressure red lined, and I got light headed when I started hyperventilating like a McDonnell Douglas wind tunnel. A little pool of sweat formed in my free hand as my right hand put a death grip on the instrument that brought the devastating news that the date may slip away. I could see the expensive flowers withering at the florist, and all the deposits with wings attached flying out of my wallet. Not to mention the fact that my daughter, graduate student at NYU, was still to a certain degree "on the payroll" and I was counting the days (W minus 14) until getting a significant pay raise. I had visions of Martin Luther King talking directly to me in that famous speech, "Free at last, free at last . . . not so fast, Farrell!"

I guess, in retrospect, I should have shown more sympathy and concern for Mark's well-being, since he is a terrific guy we think very highly of. I do know in my heart that I thought all the right things and I had honorable intentions. But it remains a fact that my opposing side has never let me forget that the first words out of my mouth inquired, "Can he still say 'I do'?" I will also have to admit, as much as I hate to, that my daughter's answer, "Yes," sounded more beautiful than Celine Dion on Dolby and that those couple of seconds between asking the question and hearing the response seemed more than a lifetime, as I envisioned my entire net worth, anorexic and getting skinnier by the flower, flash before my eyes.

The song for the first dance was changed from "It Had To Be You" to "Falling For You." The honeymoon had to be postponed, but otherwise the wedding went as planned: Mark hobbled down the aisle on his crutches and married Allison, and off they went to live happily ever after. Tough way to earn it, but he has gotten a lifetime exemption from cleaning the roof!

$ $$ $$$

Flowers fall into one of those categories that fathers of the bride don't pay much attention to as plans progress. Kinda like driving down the road and your wife says, "Look at the pretty flowers." You usually grunt something like, "Lovely, just lovely," thinking it unsafe for her to direct your attention away from driving while listening to Curt Schilling trying to wrap up a no-hitter. Everyone knows that men are incapable of doing more than one other thing while driving, and looking at flowers definitely does *not* make the list today . . . and it's not looking too good for tomorrow either!

As we scan the wedding landscape, we get so concerned about the cake, dress, photography, and food that we sometimes unintentionally let the flowers slip through the blooming crack. Don't be pump faked by the silence of the opposing side in regard to flowers. They may not know much in the beginning, but they become "chapter and verse" bona fide botanical experts by the end, the main tidbit of knowledge being how criminally expensive flowers are. Brothers in the Society, your wampum can get absolutely torched by the cost of a freeze-dried, hand-tied Stephanotis and Amaryllis Biedermeier. You better have your sonar on high gain when "flowers begin to bloom!" Think about the "flower pot" as being a fondue pot and think of the meat that goes in as your money. No matter how big the money when it goes in, it comes out a *whole* lot smaller.

Your primary recourse: "It's sad so many beautiful flowers get whacked and die for such a short use. I read somewhere, in *two* places actually, that environmentally conscious brides lean more and more toward renting silk flowers." Your chance here: a paltry 0.7 on the WPS; but you never know—odds in the lottery really suck but there is a winner!

One last word of advice: Don't pick wildflowers from the interstate thinking you might save a little money. It constitutes a federal offense to do so, and it would be truly embarrassing for you to land in the slammer on the big day. Of course, if this happens you only need to qualify for "wedding release" fifteen minutes prior to kickoff because you won't be missed until then.

Stop and smell the roses!!

Thirteen

$\mathcal{S}$omeone described the way you get comfortable with the money you have to spend and thereby decelerate the jaws of the Hassle Factor Index. First, you sashay on down to your bank with a big ol' gunny sack and cram it full of one-hundred-dollar bills. Then ease on home and start flushing them down the toilet, one at a time, until you become completely at ease and it doesn't bother you anymore. If this sounds like fun, go get a big handful of crisp new ones with Ben Franklin on the front, grab hold of that solid brass handle on your American Standard and start pumping!

"NOW TO PHOTOGRAPHY"

Not a Kodak moment. No self-respecting bride would ever stoop so low as to have her picture taken by a Kodak. At the very least you need a Hasselblad medium format 500 CM with 80mm lens and Metz 60-CT4 flash, or a Canon EOS IV with 28-80 F2.8 lens with 550 Ex flash, or a Nikon D-1X three-frames-per-second 5.4 million pixels and SB-80 flash. And of course the only people on earth who could possibly know how to use such equipment—"professional wedding photographers." In fact some believe (not denied by professional wedding photographers), that *only* professional wedding photographers can by law own such equipment. I don't want to demean a whole profession, but I want you to know some of these photographers aren't playing with a full set of lenses.

It's a good bet that if you put one of those fancy Nikons in the hands of a chimpanzee, then have it walk around and take a thousand pictures, you *will* get, by dumb luck, a hundred keepers. Or hide a camera between the third and fourth tiers of the nine-tier cake and have it automatically take a picture every five seconds. I'll bet three rolls of Fuji Super HQ 100 film that you get enough good ones to fill that $250 leather Gucci wedding album.

You may hear the bride say that to get good pictures she needs to form a "warm personal relationship" with the photographer—they need to "bond." Any

photographer who forms a warm personal relationship with forty brides a year is suspect and should be
avoided. Eighty percent of the cost goes for the
"bonding" and 20 percent for the pictures! Since when
does a warm personal relationship have anything to do
with the quality of the pictures? I'll bet two 8 x 10
glossies of Shamu that the photographer who shot that
famous picture of Muhammad Ali standing over a
decked Sonny Liston didn't have a "warm personal
relationship" with the Champ. Get real!

One of the main problems with photography is the
candid (read embarrassing) photos that may develop
(pun intended). The following e-mail illustrates in living Polaroid 600 color the risk inherent in letting a
photographer loose at your wedding.

Princess@fabwedding.com

Dear Princess,

*I do think the name Princess fits my favorite
niece and I hope you will keep it and not go back
to Matilda. Someone with your spunk and charisma
deserves a royal title.*

*Your leaving a fabulous wedding via jet helicop-
ter, streaming red, white, and blue smoke, from the
eighteenth hole at Pebble Beach was nothing short
of spectacular. I saw Tiger Woods "fly in" to the
eighteenth at the US Open, but I have never seen
anyone "fly out!" I trust your honeymoon in Bora*

Bora provides many special memories. Joe-Bob sure lucked out and I wish him the best in the bait and tackle business in Monterrey.

I want to share some concern over the wedding proofs your Mom showed me just a few moments ago. With a mixture of pride and reservation, I had her promise not to show them to anyone else until I could correspond with you. I will say the quality of the photos is indeed fantastic, as I would expect from a photographer named DeMille who lives in Hollywood.

As you know, photographs can be misleading and certainly give the wrong impression on occasion. I am afraid this happened in three of the pictures. I hope you will consider deleting these from your album and certainly encourage you not to get reprints of these particular ones. In fact, I will pay a handsome sum of money if you could secure the negatives for me (contract enclosed). Especially troubling is the appearance some of these portray given the fact that your Aunt Grace could not attend the wedding with me because she volunteered to give the keynote address for the Women Against Feminism annual conference in Waco, Texas, that weekend. Her speech, warmly received, on "Manners and Etiquette of the Sensitive Man" gives further concern reference these pictures.

The first picture that gives pause is the one of me with that young lady whose name I can't remember in front of the ice carving of the horse.

Although it appears I am looking down her dress, I can positively say I was just trying to help find her Harry Winston diamond earring that fell off and disappeared down her extremely low-cut dress. I know the smile on my face looks mischievous, but I can assure you I had honorable intentions.

The second picture of concern is the one of Joe-Bob's aunt and me in the garden beneath the grape arbor. Being almost totally dark, the surprised look on my face came from the blinding flash of the camera, not from the fact that my arms appear to be around her waist. I thought she had tripped and I just tried to save her from falling in the pond with those nasty giant Kois.

The third shows me and your sorority sisters in the fountain in front of the country club. I know the clock on the stone entrance shows 3:00 A.M., but surely it must have been broken because I haven't been up that late since Neil Armstrong walked on the moon. The fact that your sorority sisters, especially Sophia, were in various states of undress at the moment the photo snapped totally disguises the truth. Playing Good Samaritan, I surely saved them from drowning since demon rum had apparently taken hold.

Although I haven't seen the video I ask you to be on the lookout for one potentially embarrassing shot. After the reception I went, against my will, to Captain Harry's Bar, Deli and Fireworks Emporium. Had I ever conceived the next turn of events, I cer-

*tainly would not have gone and I must confess to
being shocked by the behavior of some in the wedding party. After being forced to belt down three
or four tequila shooters I somehow ended up with
Sandy's Triple D Wonder Bra on my head. The last
thing I remember is someone yelling "Roll the film!"
and being temporarily blinded by a two-million-can-
dlepower light. When the light went out I recog-
nized your videographer with his Sony Digital XL 500
professional grade triple zoom mini-cam and enor-
mous grin on his face.*

*Ever since my Navy days and an unfortunate inci-
dent at the old Cubi Point Officers Club in the
Philippines, I have believed that whiskey and cam-
eras pose a risky combination that can lead to some
false presumptions. I know I can depend on my favorite
niece to look out for her favorite uncle in this sensitive time.*

*A little check will arrive shortly to help defray
some expenses of your honeymoon. I look forward to
hearing from you soon and wish you and Joe-Bob the
best. By the way, I would appreciate the name and
number of your videographer, as I have a special
project I want to talk with him about. Would you
please e-mail me that ASAP?*

*Love,
Uncle Henry*

*** WARNING ***

If you have spirits and a video camera at the reception, there *will* be some embarrassing footage (9.8 on the WPS). I strongly recommend you make sure you're not in it!

You may think that after the reception, spending ends. Not exactly. A month later the proofs arrive. The opposing side gets one last jolt of residual Hysteriamone and they relive the glorious evening in living Kodachrome color via the video and albums. Whatever you budgeted for photography will be significantly increased (9.9 on the WPS) as they purchase extra 3x5's, 5x6's, and 8x10's to send to every single person who was photographed, which includes about 99 percent of the attendees—a classic boat/airplane moment.

$$ $$$

The best you can hope for is that the opposing side will allow a friend with a 35mm Minolta SLR, a professional wedding photographer "wannabe," to volunteer his time and you pay for the film (0.8 on the WPS). Or you can put about fifteen of those instamatic throw-aways on the tables so people can take their own pictures. If the truth be known, these "toys" can get some of your best shots.

The worst case scenario forces you to spend a ton of money on something very similar to an exercise bike. You nearly wear the bike out for about two weeks and a year down the road it becomes an expensive tie rack. How many times in the last twenty years have you sat down and looked at your wedding pictures? A visual reminder of the glorious day lights up the opposing side, ranking a close second in excitement to the wedding dress.

When you lose control, take it like a man!

You have just completed a financial disaster triple play—dress to flowers to photography, if you're scoring at home. Now in the bottom of the ninth, the opposing side has the bases loaded and the mother of all home run hitters, Mark Bonsosa, steps to the plate with grand slam on his mind!

Fourteen

WARNING

*R*eading this chapter may cause some, most, or all of the following: high blood pressure, irregular heartbeat, hypertension, stress, insomnia, gastrointestinal disorders, mood swings, and involuntary increased consumption of alcohol and/or Prozac. This chapter may cause a premature crossing of the lines in the Hassle Factor Index or, at the least, will cause a rapid acceleration. Certain drugs such as Viagra could be rendered ineffective. Fathers of the bride should consult their physicians before reading. Research has shown no side effects on others.

You have now reached the big time. Everything up to this point has been minor league, trivial, inconsequential, picayune, minute, and/or miniscule. You have just jumped into the deep end!

LET'S TALK RECEPTION!!!

If you think for a second that the dress, flowers, and photography will vaporize your golden goose, you probably should skip this chapter because the simoleon metabolic rate of the reception makes all other expenditures look like a gnat on a water buffalo. This end of the whip could very well be your financial Waterloo, an event that could cause your net worth to come out with a sheet over it.

Let's put this in proper perspective: Think about going to a very expensive restaurant. You haven't eaten all day, one click short of ravenous, and you order a big steak for about thirty bucks. You have been waiting anxiously for forty-seven minutes, according to your trusty Timex, bought recently instead of the Seiko Sports Chronometer you always wanted. Your tank is darn near empty, one click _past_ ravenous. You see your smiling waiter carrying your steak under a covered silver dish held over his head, like a torchbearer at the Olympics. You salivate like a black Lab at suppertime, and in your mind you can see, smell, and taste the superb medium-rare meat and sense the nutriment coursing through your veins, bringing you back from your close encounter with emaciation. The waiter places the dish in front of you, from the right side of course, and proudly raises the lid to reveal a steak about the size of a sand dollar. You think maybe there has been a mistake, so you politely ask the waiter if this might be the hors d'oeuvre, to which he replies, rather indignantly, with his little white napkin draped pretentiously over his arm, "It's not the *quantity* sir, it's the *quality* that counts."

You immediately think that you have an opportunity today, right here at this very moment, to enhance the quality of society's gene pool. You resist the temptation but envision your hands around his little gold-chained neck. You respond, with stomach growling like a bear on his first posthibernation day, "I don't care if it's the highest quality meat ever carved off the rear end of a blue ribbon Santa Gertrudis from the King Ranch, I WANT A STEAK!" You start figuring the cost per pound of this little morsel, and you come to the conclusion that it costs about the same as an hour of time from your high-powered attorney.

When you start figuring reception costs, stand by. The problem persists that total cost equals a bunch more than one hour from your high-priced attorney; think about hiring your attorney for a long time, I mean a *real long time*. Think Johnny Cochran and the dream team on your payroll with the meter running—continuously! Help me out here.

This reception business makes the cost overruns on the B-2 bomber look like chump change. After you find out what one-half of one deviled egg costs, you'll think the Defense Department got a bargain on those nine-hundred-dollar hammers. If the wedding industry ka-chings $32 billion a year, then $31 billion is plunked down on the reception (not to rain on your parade, but you know about after-tax dollars, so the real cost exceeds $31 billion . . . plug in your tax bracket!). In the common vernacular, "THIS IS NUTS!" If you ever believed in the words "don't ask, don't tell," use them now. I promise you only one thing: If you can afford and stand not knowing the cost of the reception, add at least two years to your life.

I won't bore you with all the ins and outs of the reception—the number of moving parts on this puppy would overload an IBM mainframe. I just want to give you three scenarios that you need to have your ears tuned to because they will give you an indication early on of just how much heavy lifting you face as the opposing side runs the table. Three possible conversations that you might overhear from the opposing side follow. Each corresponds to $, $$, or $$$.

$

Mother of the Bride: "I really think some assorted cheeses, finger sandwiches, meatballs, and some fruit like apples, bananas, and oranges would be terrific."

Bride: "That sounds great. And since the reception is in the church social hall, some nonalcoholic punch would be perfect."

Mother of the Bride: "We may have enough money for some celery and carrots. The caterer's menu says you can get celery for seven dollars a ton and dip for two dollars a gallon."

Bride: "And the church organist has agreed to play the piano at the reception for fifty dollars. She says we don't need extra flowers because she will take the flowers from the sanctuary to the social hall."

If you, as father of the bride, ever hear a conversation even remotely resembling this (0.5 on the WPS), "charmed life" doesn't do you justice. This is a slam dunk. You should hug the opposing side with great enthusiasm while saying, "You ladies amaze me with your fabulous job of planning. I can't wait for the day. By the way, I read in two different places that meatballs are people's favorite, and although expensive, you have my blessing. Make sure you order plenty, and if you can, please substitute a couple dozen of those little Buffalo wings, Extra Hot, for some of the meatballs!"

The only way you can get fricasseed with this scenario is if ten thousand people show up. With the money not spent on the reception you, a financially happy camper, can now go out and invest in (we "buy" wedding stuff; we "invest" in recreational items!) those Callaway constant-width irons (4° consistent left progression) with VFT Technology, RCH

85i Titanium Strong flex shafts, and Great Big Bertha II driver, or that brand new Orvis T3 909 2 pc. mid flex ultra-high modulus graphite fly fishing rod with the thermoplastic-enriched resins, or that Harley Davidson Heritage Softail with custom spoked wheels, screaming eagle pipes, high performance air intakes, thunderheader, and leather saddle bags. You, in Fat City, just dodged the ultimate Hi Yo Silver-tipped financial bullet, the lines of the Hassle Factor Index have taken a *rapid* deceleration, and you are sitting pretty in the saddle here on the backstretch.

Of course being a good businessman you know, "If it ain't in writing, it ain't!" It would pay you to get this matter under contract ASAP, PDQ, immediately! Time, *definitely* of the essence, makes it critical to get this thing wrapped up, because if you don't and the gestation period lingers, the opposing side may go to the fancy wedding of a friend, which may lead to a little jealousy and one-upswomanship. Or, they may go to one of those Bridal Showcases and get cornered by the Hilton's director of sales, a woman of immense sincerity and sales ability. She gets them to sign on the dotted line and makes your golf sticks, fishing gear, and Harley disappear like dimpled chads in Dade County.

So, your last comment should be: "And by the way, I read in two different places about a price increase on food due to the drought, so you better go ahead and get the contracts signed so you can lock in the good prices. If you do that now you may save enough money to buy that nice veil you talked about. And since my job entails a lot of contracts, I would be more than happy to go with you to make sure we cover all the details [note "we"]. Would tomorrow morning at seven-thirty suit or would early afternoon be better?" Although very difficult, you must try to contain your zeal on this last comment lest they become suspicious. The opposing side, very perceptive, becomes wary if their hypersensitive antennas sense your enthusiasm about *any* expenditure of money.

$$

Bride: "The Virginia Ham Biscuits sound delicious. Right next to it we will have several spreads for the English wafers. The folks at the Holiday Inn seem most knowledgeable."

Mother of the Bride: "Yes, and I just love crab, pâté, and vegetable spread—and some encrusted Brie would complement them beautifully."

Bride: "We need some fruit for the chocolate fondue, like strawberries, apples, and bananas."

Mother of the Bride: "Yummy, and we need something substantial to eat since we will have beer and wine for two hours, so how about roast beef with a variety of breads?"

Bride: "Terrific. The florist offered to discount a large arrangement for the serving table where we hold the wedding toast with sparkling wine."

Mother of the Bride: "I almost forgot, Katherine called last night and said her brother, a real character and disc jockey on station WKQR, has agreed to do the music."

Bride: "I've seen him; he's really good. One other thought: Since the church is so close to the Holiday Inn, could we rent a van to transport the wedding party to the reception?"

Mother of the Bride: "Sure, and your Dad's good friend Walker Stewart has volunteered his new Lexus to take you and Tom to the reception."

If you hear this conversation, your cash position faces serious danger, the magnitude of which depends on how many people come to the wedding. If 50 people attend, you can survive it. Between 50 and 150 you might consider yourself "on the bubble." Over 150 and it's a major assault, net worth definitely in harm's way, a serious financial mugging. The only remedy here is to attempt a limit on the number of people ("I read somewhere that as weddings become more personal, only family and real close friends receive invitations") or scale back on the menu ("I read somewhere that roast beef, because of Mad Cow Disease, should be replaced with chicken wings").

$$\$\$\$$$

If you haven't overheard either the $ or $$ scenario, one of two things has happened: either you have not been around much because of your travel schedule, or the opposing side has conspired against you and joined together in a Mafia-like Weddingate partnership of silence and deception. They have in fact been holding $$$ conversations under a Code Red level of security, hoping to skip this budget buster past you like a Stealth bomber behind an Afghan sand dune. You're playing hardball with the big dogs now!

Mother of the Bride: "This sounds delicious: Tequila Cured Jumbo Gulf Shrimp sliced paper thin, served on Alaskan Crab Cake garnished with authentic Russian Caviar and Pommes Souffles Lettuce, grilled asparagus with Three Kings Goat Cheese, oysters on the half shell, Peking Duck stuffed with marinated artichoke hearts, whole salmon glazed with papaya salsa, Japanese eggplant and Kobe beef."

Bride: "I can't wait to hear the bands. The jazz band won the North American Jazz Festival, and the twenty-piece orchestra backed up Billy Joel at Caesar's Palace in Las Vegas."

Mother of the Bride: "I don't know much about drinks, but the selection sure sounds impressive— Tanquery, Glinfiddich, Courvoisier Reserve, Bombay, Booker's, Grey Goose, Macallan, Hennessy, Grand Marnier."

Bride: "Can you imagine a toast with five hundred of our closest friends, drinking Dom what's his name champagne? I just love the name Dom!"

Mother of the Bride: "The carriage ride from the church to Pebble Beach Country Club pulled by the Budweiser Clydesdales sounds lovely, and the artificial snow machine will make it look just like the commercials. Let's not forget to notify them about the three limos transporting the wedding party over and their need for up-front parking."

Bride: "Can you believe Mario agreed to do the ice carvings? He will arrive right after he finishes the ice carvings for the closing ceremonies of the Winter Olympics. He wants to carve three houses: my sorority house where I first met Joe-Bob, the Hearst Castle where we went on our first date, and a cute little replica of the Waffle House where we shared a western omelette with extra tomatoes, whole wheat toast with grape jelly, hash browns with catsup, and Diet Coke. Coming in to the reception guests will see a life-sized carving of Sheba, my favorite Arabian mare that I won my first blue ribbon on. She is such a special part of my life I just couldn't leave her out."

Mother of the Bride: "I've had nothing but nightmares worrying about the forklift dropping the cake, and not getting the hibiscus and fresh leis here on time from Hawaii."

If your opposing side ever holds a conversation at the $$$ level, you have lost control; their Hysteriamones have kicked into afterburner, and your fortune just got fubar'd. They view money at this stage as just another small hindrance on their way to wedding heaven. Like Secretariat coming down the stretch at The Belmont, Michael Jordan against the Knicks, Joe Montana against Dallas, or Tiger coming up the eighteenth at Augusta, they will not be denied! They smell victory, and for you to even think about getting in their way is ludicrous because they will crush you like Dumbo stepping on a five-day-old banana. This money-spending avalanche roaring down the Tetons gains momentum with each ambidextrous swipe of the VISA. "Nothing in moderation, let's do it!" becomes their battle cry. The statement "I don't know if we can afford it," last spoken one wedding millisecond after Hysteriamone raced through their bloodstream, will never be spoken or even thought of again. It has finally been confirmed that your wedcentric opposing side failed math because they buy eight of every four things needed. Your local department stores have them registered as serial spenders!

If the opposing side has taken up permanent residence in the $$$ level, I feel your pain. I can also sense your reputation: wonderful person, loving Dad, devoted husband, an honest and caring businessman; but financially you are in deep kimchi. I hope you have millions and own Boardwalk, Park Place with two hotels, and three railroads, because the chance stands at 8.2 on the WPS that after the wedding you will have to go back to work . . . on your *first* million. You are caught in a class-six rapid. You might be able to maneuver a little, but you *are* going down the river. One thing for sure: In the $$$ range, they have got you by the veils!

$ $$ $$$

It really doesn't make any difference which level of spending you find yourself; it's all relative. The reception, Super Bowl of expenditures, a notorious place where many a good father of the bride has met his monetary maker, has only one redeeming feature —it signals the last major sucking sound your Fort Knox will hear.

The reception represents the ultimate test of your fiscal manhood. You can throw in the towel and plead "no mas," or you can look the grim financial reaper in the eye and assert, "You may obliterate my net worth all the way to the obituary column and make me drink Ripple wine and eat Doritos the rest of my days; you may cause me to drive my recently purchased four-year-old Hyundai 200,000 miles, sell my Grady White with Honda Four Stroke, and fish from the bank with dug-out-of-my-own-yard worms instead of those seductive shiners I get from Bubba's Bait and Tackle Shop on Highway 378 right past the new Wal-Mart; you might make me read the *Wall Street Journal* online and cancel *Sports Illustrated* even before the annual swimsuit issue; oh, yes, and force me to scuba dive for golf balls on the sixteenth hole at the municipal course and swap my behind-home-plate for right-field-upper-deck seats for opening day of my beloved Cubbies; or coerce me into selling my V-8 automatic transmission with overdrive and two TV-VCRs Winnebago Warrior motorhome to pay for the maxed out VISA, MasterCard, American Express, and Discover. You may do all these things, but you will *never, ever* make me lose the will to live."

Stand up! Get that swagger back and convey a little narcissistic in-your-face Jordanesque financial trash talk. You, the captain of your ship, kick some butt! Be proud, confident, positive . . . and broke!

* * * *

Is it any wonder that the person who invented weddings never stepped forward to take credit!

Fifteen

*J*ust in case your title is "father of the groom" and you read this book with a smug feeling of prosperity and hubris running rampant, I think it's appropriate to give you a few tips on how to maintain good relations with the father of the bride. It probably will never come up in conversation, but an unspoken icy coolness may settle in between the two of you concerning the money factor. You know, the father of the bride knows, and the father of the bride knows that you know that you have got the best end of this deal. Don't offer any words of sympathy. Just pony up for the rehearsal dinner, fifteen or twenty bucks per person for barbecue and beer, and have a great time the next day at the wedding (not to mention that the number of people at the wedding *far* exceeds those at the rehearsal dinner).

If you, as father of the groom, also have a daughter, then the father of the bride will let you skate by on this, figuring, rightly so, that you have paid your dues or will pay your dues soon enough. You are, in fact, in the brotherhood, a father of a bride and a member in good standing of the KWOMS Society. However, if your groom-to-be son has no sister, then the father of the bride looks upon you as one lucky cowboy who doesn't have a clue what a terrible financial situation the father of the bride finds himself in (KWOMS Society research shows that men who have daughters retire with 12 percent less net worth per daughter than men who have only sons). You also need to know that this man with Hassle Factor Lines accelerating faster than the bullet train from Tokyo to Osaka is probably doing research on who came up with this insane notion that the father of the bride pays for everything. The father of the bride secretly hopes the government gets involved here and passes a law (he has written his congressman) that makes fathers of brides and grooms share the cost equally (KWOMS Society has formed a PAC!). You can believe that if flu shots for kids cost $32 billion there would be some congressional action! And by the way, where the heck is Ralph Nader hiding when we really need him?

There's a pretty good chance Eve came up with this cockamamie idea. I can hear her now, "Look, Adam, having a baby is tough duty, and I did most of the work raising the children while you ran through the woods selling those patented hickory, inlaid-with-teak clubs. I will see this through to the end so I refuse to leave my daughter's wedding [note "my"] to a no-load Dad of some young man who doesn't know a tiara from a peacock feather boa. Henceforth and forever more you bear the responsibility for making the money and I decide how to spend it! Now get back out there on your new dinosaur and sell some more clubs. We need a little jingle so we can replace Evy's loin cloth with one of those new wedding gowns."

Adam, hopping up on Tyranny, replied, "OK, but please hold the line on the reception; the grass hut holds only fifty people."

"Fine," she said sharply, with pursed lips, hands on hips, and wide eyes. "By the way, you know the wedding celebration kicks off on the same day as the finals of the dinosaur roping contest, the only day we could get the Vine Swingers Jungle Drum Band, so you can't enter this year. And one other thing: When you ride by that garden, stop and pick some fruit off the tree!"

It's been downhill for fathers of the bride ever since!

One other piece of historical evidence about this conspiracy of the opposing side: KWOMS Society research has uncovered proof that Delilah, irate with Samson's refusal to lighten up on the purse strings for their daughter's wedding (something about an extra chariot), cut his hair while he slept, thus zapping his strength to resist, and then sold their only cow for cash, thereby coining (no pun intended) a phrase for all time. Delilah got the extra chariot *and* a shark's tooth necklace (the rage at the time) to go with her leopard-skinned backless dress.

Whether Eve, Delilah, or someone a generation or two later, the precedence is set: The father of the bride has been anointed the "Bovine de Doubloon." The bottom line: You, the father of the groom, don't have to worry about your wallet, but you do have to keep your mouth shut. Read very carefully the Top Ten List from the home office in Wagner, South Dakota, of things that you *never* want to say to the father of the bride:

10. "I can't wait to see the fourteen-tier cake."
9. "Do you mind if I invite my slow-pitch winter softball team?"
8. "I had three brothers and I have two sons. Lucky, huh?"
7. "Can you believe the barbecue for the rehearsal party is $8.95 per person? Outrageous!"
6. "I'd always heard raising girls cost more."
5. "How will you park six hundred people?"

4. "Renting a tuxedo is really expensive."
3. "My other son's reception was at the Hilton. You sure you want to use the Holiday Inn?"
2. "I can't believe that Jason came up with 250 people to invite. He never had many friends growing up."

And the number 1 thing you should NEVER say to the father of the bride:
1. "I heard you're paying for the wedding with your Enron stock."

When I had my initial flight in my first fighter squadron, the flight lead was a crusty old Great Santini-type major who had more flight time than I had alive time. I asked him what he wanted me to do as his wingman. He said, without hesitation, "Gear up, join up, keep up, and shut up!"

Not bad advice for the father of the groom.

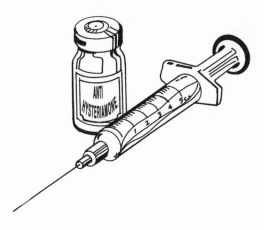

Sixteen

To a bride-to-be or mother of the bride: A well-known medical fact, documented throughout this book, clearly states that you have a large amount of Hysteriamone 1 or 2 pulsating through your veins. Not so well known is the KWOMS Society research proving that *any* members of the opposing side who have come in contact with the bride or the mother of the bride have, by proximity, a small amount of Hysteriamone 1 or 2 in their systems. Research also shows that reading certain material causes a rapid spike in Hysteriamone that can be injurious to your physical, mental, and/or financial well-being.

Because of the controversial nature of the rest of this last chapter, it is necessary to prevent anyone with Hysteriamone from accidentally reading it. Therefore, all writing after this paragraph is coated with anti-Hysteriamone vaccine that makes the writing invisible to you. We hope you, as a member of our highly respected and beloved opposing side, appreciate that our KWOMS Society precaution is offered out of concern for your safety and well-being. We wish you the best.

* * * *

OK, guys, listen up! I hated to do the aforementioned to the opposing side, but I need to tell you something in total confidence that I don't want them to see. If they ever get a hint that we are going soft, we, fathers of the bride, millions strong, lifelong card-carrying members of the award-winning KWOMS Society, are in some deep, serious trouble—more trouble than we need.

First, thank you for reading this book, because it may help defray some of the costs of my own daughter's wedding (they would have to chop down a whole bunch of trees to put much of a dent in it!). Hopefully in this somewhat truthful but mostly fun book something might help you now or in the future, like the chapter on behavioral styles. I hope you have enjoyed reading it as much as I enjoyed writing it.

My last shot of advice for you as father of the beautiful bride: This is an important day for all of you, especially your daughter and her Mom. I can't explain the opposing side's tendency for overexuberance; it's a woman thing, just as whizzing outdoors, duck hunting, deep-sea fishing, and Monday Night Football are men things. But don't win the battle and lose the war over a little money. Remember, the survey said that most people don't like to go to weddings. You can change that by giving them a good show! A good show means a good time and a great reception. A lot of your friends will take time out from their personal lives, on a weekend no less, to get dressed up and come to your party. You may have more than a few coming from across your state or even across the country. Three friends of my son-in-law came from out of the country! Some of these special people will spend a thousand dollars or more and the whole day or more to show their love and support for you, the mother of the bride and, of course, your daughter and her future husband. The least you can do is show them your appreciation. It may cost more than you expect. No, it *will* cost more than you expect. You just need to repay their friendship with more than a baloney sandwich and wine out of a box.

I don't know exactly what constitutes a "good show," and I wouldn't presume to say how much you *and* the mother of the bride should spend. Very few people have unlimited budgets, so just do the best you can for your wonderful daughter, that future son-in-law, and the family and friends who come. If you do, I promise at the end of a long, exciting, and emotional day, when you finally put your head on the pillow, you will be one proud Daddy. Good luck!

To order this book or
Charlie's first book, *Courage To Lead*,
contact Falcon Books
888-299-7568
803-407-6619
Fax 803-407-3109
www.charliefarrell.com

The Abilene Paradox

KWOMS

In some of my leadership programs we discuss how to manage disagreements (dispute resolution). Dr. Jerry Harvey, a brilliant professor and consultant, who wrote *The Abilene Paradox*, says that organizations often have an equally hard time managing agreement, which can cause major problems.

I have often mentioned *The Abilene Paradox* in my work. As I was writing this book it seemed to me that families in the throes of a wedding experience the same problem, especially surrounding the fact that we agree to invite people we really don't want to invite, and some of these same people agree to attend when they really would rather not.

I called Dr. Harvey, a most gracious individual, and talked with him about this. Although he had never considered these particular circumstances, he agreed that this situation could, in fact, be an "Abilene Paradox." He encouraged me to use it in the book if appropriate. Special thanks to Dr. Harvey, whose theory is a business classic I know you'll enjoy.

The Abilene Paradox:

The July afternoon in Coleman, Texas (population 5,607) was particularly hot—104 degrees as measured by the Walgreen's Rexall Ex-Lax temperature gauge. In addition, the wind was blowing fine-grained West Texas topsoil through the house. But the afternoon was still tolerable—even potentially enjoyable. There was a fan going on the back porch; there was cold lemonade; and finally, there was entertainment. Dominoes. Perfect for the conditions. The game required little more physical exertion than an occasional mumbled comment, "Shuffle 'em," and an unhurried movement of the arm to place the spots in the appropriate perspective on the table. All in all, it had the makings of an agreeable Sunday afternoon in Coleman—that is, it was until my father-in-law suddenly said, "Let's get in the car and go to Abilene and have dinner at the cafeteria."

I thought, "What, go to Abilene? Fifty-three miles? In this dust storm and heat? And in an unairconditioned 1958 Buick?"

But my wife chimed in with, "Sounds like a great idea. I'd like to go. How about you, Jerry?" Since my own preferences were obviously out of step with the rest I replied, "Sounds good to me," and added, "I just hope your mother wants to go."

"Of course I want to go," said my mother-in-law. "I haven't been to Abilene in a long time."

So into the car and off to Abilene we went. My predictions were fulfilled. The heat was brutal. We were coated with a fine layer of dust that was cemented with perspiration by the time we arrived. The food at the cafeteria provided first-rate testimonial material for antacid commercials.

Some four hours and 106 miles later we returned to Coleman, hot and exhausted. We sat in front of the fan for a long time in silence. Then, both to be sociable and to break the silence, I said, "It was a great trip, wasn't it?"

No one spoke.

Finally, my mother-in-law said, with some irritation, "Well, to tell the truth, I really didn't enjoy it much and would rather have stayed here. I just went along because the three of you were so enthusiastic about going. I wouldn't have gone if you all hadn't pressured me into it."

I couldn't believe it. "What do you mean 'you all'?" I said. "Don't put me in the 'you all' group. I was delighted to be doing what we were doing. I didn't want to go. I only went to satisfy the rest of you. You're the culprits."

My wife looked shocked. "Don't call me a culprit. You and Daddy and Mama were the ones who wanted to go. I just went along to be sociable and to keep you happy. I would have had to be crazy to want to go out in heat like that."

Her father entered the conversation abruptly. "Hell!" he said.

He proceeded to expand on what was already absolutely clear. "Listen, I never wanted to go to Abilene. I just thought you might be bored. You visit so seldom I wanted to be sure you enjoyed it. I would have preferred to play another game of dominoes and eat the leftovers in the icebox."

After the outburst of recrimination we all sat back in silence. Here we were, four reasonably sensible people who, of our own volition, had just taken a 106-mile trip across a godforsaken desert in a furnace-like temperature through a cloud-like dust storm to eat unpalatable food at a hole-in-the-wall cafeteria in Abilene, when none of us had really wanted to go. In fact, to be more accurate, we'd done just the opposite of what we wanted to do. The whole situation simply didn't make sense.